Histo

Recipes of the Highlands and Islands of Scotland

A Classic Scottish Cookbook

Compiled by
An Comunn Gaidhealach

Originally published as
"The Feill Cookery Book"

Folklore and Mythology Archive
Kalevala Books, Chicago

'S mairg a ni tarcuis air biadh. Foolish is he that despises food.

Recipes of the Highlands and Islands of Scotland:
A Classic Scottish Cookbook

Folklore and Mythology Archive and *Historic Cookbooks of the World* series editor and designer: Joanne Asala.
www.CompassRose.com.

Published by
Kalevala Books
an imprint of
Compass Rose Technologies, Inc.
PO Box 409095
Chicago, IL 60640
www.CompassRose.com

Titles published by Kalevala Books are available at special quantity discounts to use as premiums and sales promotions or for academic use. For more information, please write to the Director of Special Sales, Compass Rose Technologies, Inc., PO Box 409095, Chicago, IL 60640 or contact us through our Web site, www.CompassRose.com.

ISBN: 978-1-880954-25-6

I cannot tell how the truth may be; I say the tale as 'twas said to me.
—Sir Walter Scott

COOKING UTENSILS

AT CASH PRICES.

Biggest Show and Largest Variety in the City.

Shaw, Walker & Co., CITY IRONMONGERY STORES,

14 to 22 UNION STREET, GLASGOW.

Established to Supply the Public with Goods at Smallest Possible Profit for Cash only.

Wire Egg Whisk—Small, 3d. ; Large, 4½d.

"Real Dover" Egg Beater, 4½d.

Queen's Pudding Boiler, 4 Sizes, 11d., 1/5, 1/9, 2/2.

Jelly Mould, Tinned, 7d.

"Lion" Jelly Mould with Copper Top, 1/10.

Wire Pastry Tray, 12", 11d. ; 14", 1/1 ; 16", 1/3.

THE FEILL

COOKERY BOOK.

GLASGOW:

M'NAUGHTAN & SINCLAIR, 29 CADOGAN STREET.

1907.

CONTENTS.

PREFACE.

"Is math an còcair an t-acras
'S mairg a ni tarcuis air biadh,
Fuarag eòrn 'ann' sàil mo bhròige,
Biadh a b' fhearr a fhuair mi riamh."

Hunger is a good cook,
Foolish is he that despises food,
Gruel of barley in the sole of my shoe,
The best food ever I got.

AFTER the defeat of Inverlochy (1431) the Earl of Mar, wandering through Lochaber, underwent great privations, and meeting one day a poor woman in Glen Roy, asked her for some food. She gave him all she had, a handful of barley, whereupon he sat down by the side of the burn, Allt Acha na Beithich, took off one of his shoes, and mixed the meal in it with water from the stream. He is then said to have made the above verse. The first two lines are as true to-day as when they were first spoken; how far we are from sharing the opinions expressed in the last two, the pages of this book will show.

The Compiler wishes to thank all those who have so very kindly helped, either by contributing recipes or advertisements, to make this book a success, and to express her obligation to Miss Watson for her ready permission to use the Tables of Weights and Measures and Provisions in Season from the Samaritan Cookery Book, and to Mr. Mackay for leave to copy Gaelic recipes from his excellent little book, "Highland Cookery."

All proceeds from the sale (after paying expenses) will be devoted to the funds of the Highland Association, and it is hoped that those who may find this little book useful will recommend it to their friends, and thus advance a good cause.

Folklore and Mythology Archive

OBJECTS OF THE HIGHLAND ASSOCIATION.

THE HIGHLAND ASSOCIATION (or An Comunn Gaidhealach) was formed in the year 1891, and has the following objects in view:—

1. To promote the cultivation of the Gaelic language and Gaelic literature, music, art and industries, by such means as the Association may from time to time determine.

2. To encourage the teaching of the Gaelic language.*

3. To propagate a knowledge of Gaelic history and culture, especially in schools.

4. To hold an annual gathering, termed " Am Mòd Gaidhealach," at which competitions in conformity with the objects of the Association shall take place, and prizes be awarded.

All true Highlanders are cordially invited to become members of the Comunn, † and thus not only help to hasten the disappearance of the present unjust educational treatment of Gaelic-speaking children, but take their part in perpetuating some of the best and most characteristic features of Highland life.

---

* Lack of space prevents fuller details being given here, but anyone desirous of further information (and also those who are still unconvinced of the usefulness of the Comunn's objects) are referred to a pamphlet, entitled "The Teaching of Gaelic in Highland Schools," published by Henry Young & Sons, South Castle Street, Liverpool. Price 3d.

† Intending members should apply to the General Secretary, Mr. JOHN MACKINTOSH, Solicitor, Inverness. The terms of membership are:—

Life Member, one subscription of	£2 2 0
Ordinary Member, an annual subscription of ...	0 5 0
Affiliated Societies and Branches, ...	1 0 0

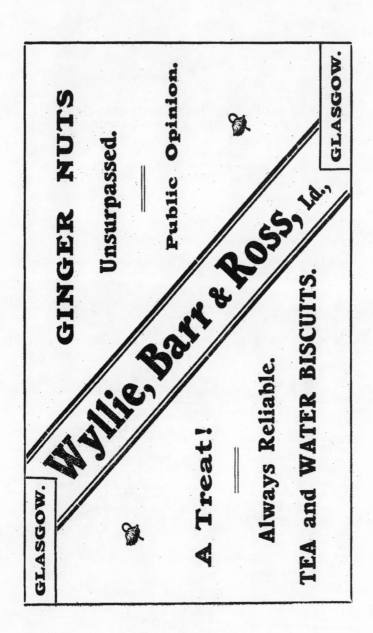

GINGER NUTS

Unsurpassed.

Public Opinion.

GLASGOW.

GLASGOW.

Wyllie, Barr & Ross, Ld,

A Treat!

Always Reliable.

TEA and WATER BISCUITS.

Folklore and Mythology Archive

Useful Weights & Measures.

¼ lb. Breadcrumbs	measures	1 Breakfastcupful.
¼ lb. Flour	,,	1 Teacupful.
1 lb. Sugar, Rice, etc.,	,,	3 Small Teacupfuls.
2 oz. Butter	,,	1 Tablespoonful.
1 oz. Dry	,,	1 Small Tablespoonful.

LIQUIDS.

4 Saltspoonfuls	measure	1 Teaspoonful.
2 Teaspoonfuls	,,	1 Dessertspoonful.
4 Teaspoonfuls	,,	1 Tablespoonful.
1 Small Teacupful	,,	1 Gill.
2 Small Breakfastcupfuls	,,	1 Pint.
4 Small Breakfastcupfuls	,,	1 Quart.
4 Tablespoonfuls	,,	1 Wine Glassful.
12 Tablespoonfuls	,,	1 Teacupful.
½ Pint	,,	1 Tumblerful.
1 Pint	,,	1 Pound.

3 Pennies - - -	weigh -	1 Ounce.
1 Halfpenny - -	measures -	1 Inch.

PROVISIONS IN SEASON.

JANUARY, FEBRUARY, AND MARCH.

Fish.

Cod, Haddocks, Ling, Whitings, Oysters, Turbot.

Meat.

Beef, House-Lamb, Mutton, Pork, Veal, Venison.

Poultry.

Turkeys, Pullets, Pigeons, Rabbits.

Game.

Grouse, Hares, Pheasants, Wild Fowl, Woodcock.

Vegetables.

Broccoli, Brussels Sprouts, Carrots, Leeks, Celery, Parsnips, Savoys.

Fruits.

Apples, Grapes, Pears, Walnuts, Oranges, Almonds, Raisins, Dates, Prunes, Figs.

APRIL, MAY, AND JUNE.

Fish.

Cod, Flounders, Salmon, Trout, Whitings, Turbot.

Meat.

Beef, Mutton, Veal, Grass-Lamb.

Poultry.

Fowls, Chickens, Ducklings, Pigeons.

Vegetables.

Cucumbers, Lettuce, Spinach (Spring), Cabbage, Carrots, Peas, Beans, Cauliflower.

Fruits.

Apples, Pears, Rhubarb, Melons, Gooseberries, Raspberries, Strawberries, Cherries.

JULY, AUGUST, AND SEPTEMBER.

Fish.

Herring, Ling, Soles, Haddock, Flounders, Salmon, Turbot.

Meat.

Mutton, Beef, Veal, Lamb, Pork.

Poultry.

Fowls, Chickens, Geese, Ducks, Larks.

Game.

Grouse, Blackcock, Partridges, Pheasants.

Vegetables.

Cauliflower, Lettuce, Cress, Peas, Beans, Turnip, Carrot,
Tomatoes.

Fruits.

Gooseberries, Currants, Plums, Grapes, Peaches, Damsons,
Pears, Quinces, Nectarines.

OCTOBER, NOVEMBER, AND DECEMBER.

Fish.

Haddock, Oyster, Lobster, Whitings, Soles, Crabs, Plaice, Cod.

Meat.

Pork, Mutton, Beef, Veal, House-Lamb.

Poultry.

Larks, Chickens, Geese, Wild Duck, Turkey.

Game.

Pheasants, Hares, Snipe, Doe, Venison, Rabbits, Woodcock.

Vegetables.

Leeks, Celery, Onions, Parsnips, Sprouts, Beetroot, Tomatoes,
Vegetable Marrow.

Fruits.

Walnuts, Grapes, Figs, Pears, Apples, Oranges, Dates,
Crystallised Preserves, Dried Fruits.

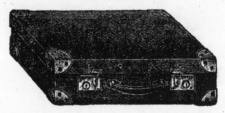
Folklore and Mythology Archive

SOUPS.

BRUSSELS SPROUT SOUP.

2 oz. butter	Brussels sprouts
1 oz. flour	Pepper and salt
Some good stock	Some cream

Melt the butter in a saucepan, add the flour, and mix well together, then the stock. Boil a few Brussels sprouts till tender, preserving the colour, rub them through a fine hair sieve, then add to the stock, already boiling, season, and add the cream before sending to table. The cream is a great improvement.

Mrs. W. E. CRUM, The Manor House, Fyfield.

CARROT SOUP.

3 carrots	1 turnip
1 onion	1 quart of water
A little butter	Pepper and salt

Grate the red part of the carrots, and cut the turnip and white part of the carrots and onion small, fry them in a little butter, and simmer gently in the water for an hour. Strain the soup over the grated carrot, add pepper and salt, and simmer all together for 20 minutes. A little cream is an improvement to this soup.

Miss HUGHES.

COCK-A-LEEKIE SOUP (for 10).

2 or 3 bunches of leeks	1 fowl (trussed for boiling)
5 quarts stock	Seasoning

Wash the leeks well (if old, scald them in boiling water). Take off the roots and part of the heads, and cut them into lengths of about an inch.   Put half the quantity into a pot with the stock and the fowl, and allow to simmer gently. In half-an-hour add the remaining leeks, and let all simmer for 3 or 4 hours longer. It must be carefully skimmed, and seasoned to taste. To serve the fowl, carve neatly, placing the pieces in the tureen and pouring over them the soup.

Mrs. W. E. CRUM, Fyfield.

CREAM OF CUCUMBER SOUP.

2 oz. lean ham
½ oz. butter
A little nutmeg
A few peppercorns
½ pint good double cream

1 teaspoonful sugar
4 cucumbers
Small ladleful white sauce
A very little good white
    stock

Put the ham (minced), butter, nutmeg, peppercorns, and cucumbers (cut up and trimmed) in a stewpan on a slow fire to simmer for 20 minutes, then add sauce, reduce quickly on a brisk stove with the stock, and when it assumes the appearance of a soft paste add cream and sugar, boil for 5 minutes longer, then rub through the tammy in the usual way, and make it hot enough in the stewpan for use.

Miss CAMPBELL of Jura.

CRÊME D'ORGE SOUP.

1 teacupful pearl barley
1 oz. butter
1 onion
½ pint milk

Small bit mace
2 yolks of eggs
Small bit cinnamon
2 quarts white stock

Wash barley and put in a saucepan with the stock, add onion, mace, and cinnamon. Let all simmer 3 hours. Strain, and rub through sieve. Return stock to saucepan to boil. Add butter, beat yolks and milk together, and add some of the soup to them gradually. Remove saucepan from fire, and pour the warmed yolks into the soup. Season and serve.

Mrs. GEORGE BROWN, Châlet Fairlie, Pau.

FISH SOUP.

Put the bones, trimmings, and skin of any fish you may have into the liquor in which fish has boiled, with a suitable assortment of vegetables and flavouring herbs, a few peppercorns, and a little spice, and boil the whole for a couple of hours. Strain it off, add to each quart an ounce of boiled rice, a teacupful of milk, and $\frac{1}{2}$ teaspoonful of finely-chopped parsley. Serve at once. Small pieces of fish improve the soup.

Mrs. BRODRICK,
31 Greenheys Road, Liverpool.

HARE SOUP.

A hare	4 peppercorns
3 carrots	A stick of celery, or a teaspoonful
$\frac{1}{2}$ a turnip	of celery salt
4 onions	Butter
A little bunch of thyme and parsley	

After the hare has been skinned and cleaned, and the blood saved, put it into a basin of cold water for a few minutes, then take the pieces out and dip in flour and fry in a piece of butter. Put the blood to the water in the basin, and strain into the pan with the meat, stir till it boils. Simmer for 6 or 8 hours, adding the vegetables about two hours before it is done. Take out the back when cooked, and save for cutting in dice when the soup is served.

If it is not thick enough, add a little flour and butter thickening.

BROADMEADOWS, Selkirk.

HOTCH-POTCH.

The scrag of a neck of mutton, well stewed for several hours with turnips and carrots cut as for broth, a quart of shelled peas (which are too old to be good boiled), celery, the hearts only of cabbage. When cold skim off the fat and take out the meat; next day stew again, adding a quantity more of younger peas and some chops from the best end of the neck of mutton. The vegetables should be very plentiful in this soup. Serve in a tureen, and leave the chops in.

Mrs. CAMPBELL of Inverneill.

IMITATION HARE SOUP.

3 oz. gravy beef	1 quart water or stock
1 tablespoonful of flour	1 bay leaf
1 oz. butter	4 peppercorns
1 onion	Sprig parsley
2 cloves	1 dessert-spoonful mushroom
1 small carrot	ketchup
Small piece turnip	1 teaspoonful Worcester sauce

Cut the beef into ½-inch dice, flour them and fry in the butter till well browned, then brown the remainder of the flour. Brown the onion with cloves stuck in it. This may be done either in a hot oven or in a pan over the fire. Put all the ingredients together and simmer gently for 1½ hours. Then strain, return the meat and soup to the pan; add force meat balls, and simmer 10 minutes.

Mrs. BRODRICK,
31 Greenheys Road, Liverpool.

ITALIAN SOUP.

1 onion	Milk
A little butter	Nutmeg
A cupful of rice	Pepper
1 quart water	Salt
Parmesan or other cheese	

Slice the onion in rings and fry in the butter, add the rice and water. Boil till the rice is soft and has absorbed all the water. Thin to a proper consistency with milk. Add the grated nutmeg, pepper and salt, and serve with grated cheese.

Miss HUGHES.

MULLIGATAWNY SOUP.

Shin of beef	½ oz. coriander seed
4 large onions	5 oz. tamarac
Best part of a fowl or rabbit	½ oz. ground ginger
Flour	A small teaspoonful cayenne,
Curry powder made as follows :—	put in according to taste

Make the beef into good stock. Slice and fry the onions in butter till a light brown, dredge with flour, add the curry powder, warm a little, then add stock. Boil all together a little, then strain it through a fine sieve. Add the fowl or rabbit (cut in pieces). If not thick enough, add a little more flour.

Mrs. CAMPBELL of Inverneill.

MUSHROOM SOUP.

1 lb. of mushrooms	1 gill of cream
3 pints of brown stock	2 ozs. of butter
1 small onion	1 oz. of flour

Salt and pepper

Skin the mushrooms and slice the onion, heat half the butter and fry in it the onion and the mushrooms 3 or 4 minutes, lift out 1 dozen of the smallest mushrooms and set them aside, add now the stock to the mushrooms and onion in the pan and also the seasoning, boil half an hour or until the mushrooms are quite soft, pour the soup through a fine sieve and rub through the pulp, put back into a pan, add the dozen small mushrooms, the flour mixed with remainder of butter into a ball, boil gently 5 minutes and pour into the tureen in which the cream has been placed, if liked a little sugar may be added.

Miss HUGHES, Beechwood.

OX CHEEK SOUP.

A hough or layer of beef	A glass of sherry
A knuckle of veal	A few stewed onions
A few slices of ham	Butter and flour
An ox head	Seasoning

Take the beef and put it in a pan with the veal, ham, some Jamaica pepper, and a few cloves, from which make some rich gravy; it must then be strained through a sieve and put into a clean pan. Have the head ready cleaned and cut, put it into the soup. It must boil very slowly for at least four or five hours. It may be thickened by putting in a bit of butter rolled in flour and the sherry, and a few stewed onions may be passed through a drainer and added to the soup. Season to taste. Skim it, and serve hot.

Miss L. M'INROY, Lude.

PALESTINE SOUP (without Meat).

2 lbs. Jerusalem artichokes	6 cloves
1 quart milk	1 onion
1 handful whole pepper	Butter, the size of an egg
A piece of mace	1 tablespoonful flour

1 gill cream

Boil the artichokes in salted water, and when quite cooked pass through a hair sieve. Boil the pepper, mace. cloves and onion in the milk; when the milk is well flavoured strain it. Then melt the butter, stir into it the flour, and gradually the milk and artichoke pulp. Boil it up, mix well, and lastly stir in the cream, adding more milk if the soup be too thick. Serve with small dice of bread fried in butter.

Mrs. BRODRICK,
31 Greenheys Road, Liverpool.

POTATO SOUP.

A couple of bones or more (leg of mutton, etc.)	1 carrot
1 onion	1 turnip
	Pan of potatoes

Boil the potatoes till tender. Boil the other ingredients in a separate pot till tender, and strain. Add mashed potatoes to the stock thus produced. Boil again some little time (5 to 10 minutes), strain, add seasoning, and simmer a few minutes before using.

BEECHWOOD.

POTATO SOUP.

1½ lb. of potatoes	½ gill of cream
1½ oz. of butter	1 quart of water
1 pint of milk	2 small onions

Small head of celery

Slice potatoes, onion, and celery, fry them in butter a light brown colour, add the water, and boil 30 minutes. Rub the pulp through a hair sieve, add the milk and cream, and salt and pepper to taste. Re-heat and serve.

Miss HUGHES, Beechwood.

RABBIT SOUP (for 16).

A few slices of ham	A blade or two of mace
4 rabbits	About ½ pint water
Parsley	Twopenny roll
Thyme	Salt and sugar to taste
6 onions	As much stock as you require soup

Cover the bottom of the stewpan with the ham, cut up the rabbits and add with the other ingredients. Let all stew on a very slow fire for about an hour, then add as much stock as you wish soup, and let it boil gently for an hour. Take out the rabbits, strip the meat from the bones, and beat in a mortar quite fine, then put it back into the soup with the crumbs of a twopenny roll; let it boil gently again for half-an-hour, and then rub through a sieve. Add a little salt and a dust of sugar.

You will find 3 rabbits ample for a party of 12.

Mrs. CAMPBELL of Inverneill.

SOUPE AU FROMAGE.

Onions	Butter
Pepper and salt	Bread

Gruyère and Parmesan cheese

Cut several onions in thin slices, brown them slowly in butter, add a very little water, salt and pepper, and cook for quarter of an hour; then add the amount of water necessary for your soup, and allow to boil. Place in a soup tureen which is very hot slices of bread alternately with layers of grated cheese; then pour in the boiling soup, and serve.

Mrs. CAMERON Lochmaben.

SOUPE À LA BONNE FEMME.

1 lettuce	1 tablespoonful flour
2 leaves sorrel	White stock or milk
1 onion	½ gill cream

A few drops lemon juice

Cut the vegetables into thin strips, about two inches long. Fry lightly, being careful not to brown. Add flour, and then gradually white stock or milk. Simmer for 1 hour, and add cream, pepper and salt, and a few drops of lemon juice. Don't let soup boil after cream is added.

Miss LENA LAMDEN,
11 Cowley Street, Westminster.

SOUPE DE SANTÉ.

2 quarts broth (made with mutton, veal or fowl)	6 cloves
Turnips	1 onion
Carrots	2 blades mace
1 head of celery	2 cabbage lettuces
	1 pint new milk

1 rusk or French roll

Stew 2 of the carrots and 2 of the turnips (sliced) and all the other ingredients, except the lettuces and milk, for two hours; then strain. Add the milk and lettuces (cut across), and some carrots and turnips, and boil up gently for 30 minutes. Put the rusk into your tureen, and pour your soup over it. BEECHWOOD.

SHEEP'S HEAD SOUP.

Liver, lights, and heart of a sheep	Whole pepper, cloves, & salt
A sheep's head	A glass of sherry
½ lb. pearl barley	4 quarts water
Turnips, carrots, celery, onions and parsley	Hard-boiled eggs
	A little flour and butter
	Browning and ketchup

Cut the liver, lights and heart into small pieces; stew well, but gently in four quarts of water, with the vegetables and barley; season with the pepper, cloves, and salt. When nearly done, put in the head (which must have been prepared, wool scalded off), and boil till tender. Take it out, and strain everything from the liquor; let it cool, skim, thicken with a little flour and butter, and add the browning and ketchup. Cut the best of head and tongue in slices, add them with the hard-boiled eggs and the sherry.

Miss L. M'INROY, Lude.

SPINACH SOUP.

1 lb. of spinach	2 cloves
1 small cucumber	1 oz. of butter
4 quarts white stock	Pepper and salt
1 small onion	1 gill of cream
1 blade of mace	1 oz. of flour

Wash and pick the spinach, have the stock boiling, drop in the spinach and cucumber; add the onion, cloves, mace, pepper and salt. Boil half-an-hour, put through a fine sieve, and rub through the pulp. Add now the butter and flour in a ball; boil up; pour over the cream and serve. Miss HUGHES.

SUMP SOUP.

½ pint split peas
½ lb. potatoes
¼ lb. carrots

Sweet herbs, celery, or celery seed

¼ lb. onions
½ lb. fresh beef
5 pints water

Take five pints (English) of water, the split peas, potatoes, carrots, and onions; let this boil for two hours, properly seasoned, then strain it. Take the beef, cut it in small pieces, and fry in a little butter. Put it into the soup and let it boil half-an-hour. Add the herbs just before it is sent to the table. Celery or celery seed is good in it.

Miss L. M'INROY, Lude.

TAPIOCA SOUP.

2 oz. tapioca
Yolks of 2 eggs

2 quarts good white stock
½ pint cream

Boil gently the tapioca and stock in a saucepan for 1 hour, then add the other ingredients. Mix well and serve.

Miss CAMPBELL of Jura.

TAPIOCA CREAM SOUP.

½ oz. French tapioca
1 yolk of egg
½ pint of cream
Onion

Celery
Turnip
Salt and pepper
1 pint water

Boil the celery, onion, and turnip in the water for an hour, then strain and boil the tapioca in the liquor till clear and thick. Beat up the yolk of egg, add the cream to it, and pour the boiling stock on it; add seasoning. If the tapioca rises to the top the egg is cooked enough.

Mrs. W. E. CRUM, Fyfield.

TOMATO SOUP.

4 oz. ham
1 onion
A little good clarified dripping
  or beef marrow
1 quart second stock or water
1 carrot
1 bay leaf

1 stick celery
A few peppercorns
1 quart fresh tomatoes (or a quart
  can of preserved tomatoes)
2 oz. butter
2 oz. flour

Cut the ham into dice and fry with the sliced onion in the dripping till nicely browned. Simmer in a pan the stock or water, with the carrot, bay leaf, celery and peppercorns for one hour, then add to it the tomatoes (if fresh they must be first stewed till tender), and again simmer three-quarters of an hour. Rub all through a sieve, add the flour and butter, stirring it over the fire till thoroughly amalgamated and smooth, continue stirring till it boils up, then season to taste, and serve with tiny dice of fried bread.

Mrs. BRODRICK,
31 Greenheys Road, Liverpool.

WHITE SOUP.

1 gill ordinary stock and about 2 quarts made up of bones of cooked meat, and boilings of rabbits, veal, or chickens

1 gill milk
Tablespoonful cream
3 tablespoonfuls flour
Some macaroni

When the stock is warm add the milk (cold) and cream ; let it boil, then add flour and macaroni (the latter previously boiled and cut in pieces). After adding these let it simmer only—or it will crack—for half-an-hour ; then serve.

Mrs. CAMPBELL of Inverneill.

ADDITIONAL RECIPES.

SCOTLAND'S
LEADING
Fishmongers & Poulterers,

SAWERS, L^{D.,}

11/17 West Howard St.,

58 & 60 West Nile St.,

GLASGOW.

BRANCH ESTABLISHMENTS.

4/10 High St. & Corn Market, BELFAST.

83/84 Bull Street., BIRMINGHAM.

OUR OWN CURING ESTABLISHMENTS AT ABERDEEN.

Folklore and Mythology Archive

FISH.

BAKED HADDOCK OR WHITING AND BLACK BUTTER.

STUFFING.—2 oz. oatmeal, 2 hard-boiled eggs, 2 oz. butter, some chopped herbs, pepper and salt, a little lemon juice.

A good-sized haddock or whiting.

Wash the fish well in salted water, and wipe quite dry. Have ready a stuffing made as above; stuff the fish and lay it in a well-greased baking tin; keep it well basted for 1 hour, and serve with black butter.

BLACK BUTTER.—4 oz. fresh butter, 1 oz. sifted flour, 2 tablespoonfuls cold water, 1 teaspoonful lemon juice. Fry the butter till almost black, sprinkle the flour in steadily till it is quite brown, add the water slowly, and stir one way. Serve very hot.

Miss E. M'INTYRE.

COLD CRAB.

1 nice crab and some spawn	Pepper
1 tablespoonful anchovy sauce	Salt
Butter	Mustard
1 pint cream	

Boil the crab for 20 minutes; when cold, pound the spawn in the mortar with a little butter, then pass it through a sieve on to a plate; take out all the meat from the crab, laying aside the poisonous parts, mince it very fine, add pepper, salt, and a little mustard, and the anchovy sauce; froth a pint of cream, add the meat and a little of the spawn; mix well together, put into paper cases, with a little more spawn on the top, and serve.

Miss CAMPBELL of Jura.

CROÛTES DE LAITANCES.

Hard roes	A few drops lemon juice
Thick Mayonnaise sauce	Prawns
Butter	Oil, pepper, salt
Bread	Vinegar
2 boiled anchovies	Picked watercress

Boil sufficient hard roes of any nice fish (loup, a French fish, or soles for preference), and allow them to cool. Fry a number of round pieces of bread a golden colour in butter, and, when cold, çoat them with the Mayonnaise sauce. Pound the roes with a piece of butter, the anchovies and lemon juice. Rub them through a hair sieve, cover the croûtes with a thick layer of the prepared roes, and put a shelled prawn, nicely seasoned with oil, etc., on the top of each. Arrange the croûtes on a napkin, and garnish with watercress and prawns in their shells.

Col. SANDBACH, Hafodunos.

FILETS DE SOLES EN RAMEQUINS.

2 small soles, filleted	½ glass of white wine, or lemon juice
1½ gills of white sauce (thick)	
1 oz. grated cheese	Some short pastry
2 whites of eggs, stiffly beaten	Pepper, salt, parsley

Line some oval moulds with short pastry, then with buttered paper, fill with rice and bake in a moderate oven for about 15 minutes, then turn rice and paper out. Fold the fillets smaller than the cases, put in a buttered baking tin, sprinkle with pepper, salt, and juice of lemon, cover with a buttered paper and bake 15 minutes in a slow oven. Bring the sauce to the boil, cover the bottom of each pastry case with sauce, add a fillet to each. Mix grated cheese and stiffly-whipped whites of eggs and wine with the remainder of the sauce; cover the fillets with this and bake in a moderate oven until set and fairly brown. Decorate with chopped parsley. Ramequin cases may be used for this instead of the pastry cases.

Mrs. RODERICK MATHESON.

FILETS DE SOLE À LA NANTUA.

1 or 2 soles, filleted		2 yolks of eggs
(Bones for stock)		Glass of white wine
Shrimps or prawns		6 oz. rice
	½ pint white sauce	

Put the fillets on buttered tin, cover with wine, sprinkle with salt, but no pepper, squeeze lemon juice, add a little fish stock, cover with greased paper, and bake in *moderate* oven 10 minutes.

SAUCE.—½ pint white sauce, to be coloured pink. Add yolks of 2 eggs, teaspoonful of lemon juice, but do not allow the mixture to boil after the eggs have been added as it will curdle.

RICE FOR BORDER.—Boil 6 oz. rice till it has absorbed 1½ pints fish stock made from the bones of fish; then press into greased border mould, steam and turn out. Put fillets of sole round it and pour sauce over and round the fish. Fill the centre with either prawns or shrimps, mixed with a little sauce.

Mrs. RODERICK MATHESON.

FISH PUDDING.

Cold fish		Salt
2 hard-boiled eggs		Anchovy sauce
A little cream		2 boiled potatoes
Pepper		2 raw eggs

Take the remains of any cold fish; pound it in a mortar with the other ingredients to a cream. Have ready a buttered basin, put the mixture in and cover with a buttered paper. Steam for three-quarters of an hour. Serve egg sauce with cream over and round the pudding when turned out.

Lady CHURCH,
130 Harley Street, London.

FISH SOUFFLÉ.

½ lb. fish (raw or cooked)		½ gill milk
2 oz. butter		2 oz. flour
	2 eggs	

Make sauce with butter, flour, and milk, add yolks and seasoning and fish, then stiffly beat the whites and add lightly, put in buttered tin and steam half an hour.

It may be baked, but in this case add a third white of egg, and bake ¼ hour. A little whipped cream added last greatly improves it.

(For Haddie Soufflé use only 4 oz. fish and 1 yolk *less*, and bake three quarters of an hour in a hot oven.)

Miss HUGHES, Beechwood.

FISH SOUFFLÉ.

5 or 6 oz. of raw whiting or other fish, finely chopped	1½ oz. of butter
3 whites of eggs, whipped stiff	1½ oz. of fine flour
	1 dessert-spoonful of cream
2 raw yolks of eggs	1½ gills cold milk
	½ teaspoonful essence of anchovy

Put the butter into a stewpan, with the flour and anchovy essence, a pinch of salt and a dust of pepper and 2 raw yolks of eggs. Mix this with rather better than 1½ gills of cold milk; stir all together over fire till the mixture boils. Remove from the fire, mix into it a dessert-spoonful of cream and 5 or 6 oz. of finely-chopped raw fish. Then mix in carefully 3 whites of eggs that have been whipped stiff. Put into a soufflé case and bake for half-an-hour.

Mrs. RODERICK MATHESON.

FLEURETTES DE HOMARD.

1 lobster	½ oz. of gelatine
2 tablespoonfuls of mayonnaise	½ gill of water
½ gill of aspic	A few drops of carmine

Chop the lobster, stir in the mayonnaise, add the gelatine (which has been melted in the water and cooled), then the aspic, and a few drops of carmine.

Put some aspic jelly in bottom of moulds, and decorate with chervil leaves and diamonds of chillies. When set, fill up with the lobster mixture. Turn out when cold, and dish on lettuce dressed with a little mayonnaise sauce, with a border of aspic chopped. Salmon may be used instead of lobster. Fluted diamond-shaped moulds are generally used.

Mrs. RODERICK MATHESON.

FRIED TROUT.

Mushrooms		Salt
Truffles		Pepper
Tomato sauce		Egg and breadcrumbs

Prepare a stuffing of mushrooms, truffles, salt and pepper, mince them well. Clean and empty the trout, fill them with this stuffing, sew them, and put them in a court bouillon. When the trout are cooked allow them to get cold, drain them well, dip in beaten-up yolk of egg and breadcrumbs, fry, and serve with tomato sauce.

COURT BOUILLON.—Water, salt, pepper, carrots, onion, thyme, bay leaf, cloves, vinegar, white wine (or half wine half water), the fish to be entirely covered.

Mrs. CAMERON,
National Bank House, Lochmaben.

To Cook Trout at a Picnic.

Clean the trout, wrap in white paper (newspaper can be used if no other is available), soak well in water, lay in hot ashes, and cover well over. When done the paper will peel off with the skin. Flat stones made hot under a fire are even better than ashes.

HADDOCK CASES.

A smoked haddock		1 oz. butter
1 gill thick cream		Bread
A little cayenne pepper		White of egg

Pound the butter and haddock (which has been cooked), pass through a sieve, add the cream and flavouring of pepper till it is a rich purée ; have ready some tiny cases of fried bread, fill with the mixture, and cover them with stiffly whipped white of egg. Bake in a slack oven till the white is crisp and of a delicate colour.

Miss CAMPBELL of Jura.

HERRINGS FRIED WITH OATMEAL.

Herrings rolled in a little coarse oatmeal instead of flour before frying are a nice change.

Folklore and Mythology Archive

LOBSTER NEUBURG.

1 lobster or more, according to number of people	Butter, the size of an egg
1 glass good sherry	2 yolks of eggs
	1 gill cream

Place a saucepan on the fire with half the butter, and as soon as it is hot add the lobster (previously boiled and cut in pieces), add the sherry, cover the pan and let it boil slowly; dilute the yolks of egg with the cream, add this to the lobster with the rest of the butter, cook it slowly, turning the whole briskly, and serve hot.

Miss CAMPBELL of Jura.

LOBSTER PUDDING.

Two lobsters	Very little mace
Whites of 2 and yolks of 3 eggs	Salt, cayenne, and nutmeg (if approved)
1 tablespoonful cream	Melted butter sauce

Take the large pieces from the claws, arrange them nicely in a well-buttered mould; chop the remainder of the lobsters well and mix them with the eggs and cream and seasoning, then add to the pieces in the mould. When the whole is well pressed down, cover it and put it into a pan of hot water on the stove for three-quarters of an hour; turn it out, and serve with good melted butter, mixed with the pea of the lobster, round it.

Mrs. CAMPBELL of Inverneill.

MAYONNAISE SOUFFLÉ OF CRAB.

The eatable part of a crab	Some nice aspic jelly
Pepper, salt	Mayonnaise sauce
Oil, vinegar	Fried breadcrumbs

Slightly butter the lining of a soufflé case, pin a band of buttered paper round rather high; whip up some nice aspic jelly, and put a little in the bottom of the lining; make a bed of mayonnaise sauce on the top of the aspic. Put in the crab (seasoned), then some more chopped aspic. It should be about three inches above the tin lining. Stand it in the ice-box until wanted. Put the lining in the case sprinkled with fried breadcrumbs, and serve with a plate of chopped aspic jelly apart.

Col. SANDBACH, Hafodunos.

OYSTER CREAM.

25 oysters	1 tablespoonful cornflour
1 pint cream	1 blade mace
1 tablespoonful butter	Salt, pepper

Put the oysters on to boil in their liquor. As soon as they come to the boil drain through a colander. Put the cream in a stewpan, rub the butter and cornflour together, and add to the cream. When boiling, add the mace and stir constantly until it thickens; then add the oysters, salt and pepper; stir till thoroughly heated, and serve.

Miss REED,

Wimblehurst, Horsham.

OYSTER SOUFFLÉ (for 10 people).

½ lb. white breadcrumbs	1 whiting
½ pint milk	3 dozen oysters
½ pint cream	A little pepper, salt, and
4 eggs	mace

Make the bread, cream, and milk into a sauce, like bread sauce, adding the pepper, salt, and mace to flavour it. When cold add the yolks of 4 eggs, the whiting which has been pounded, then the 4 whites of eggs beaten to a stiff snow, and lastly the 3 dozen oysters, which have been scalded in their own liquor (if large, cut them in two). Put in a plain mould and steam for one hour and a half.

FOR THE SAUCE.—The liquor of the oysters, about a gill of cream, a very small teaspoonful of cornflour, mace, pepper and salt. Bring to the boil, and boil for a minute or two, then pour round the soufflé. It is very good made with mushrooms instead of oysters.

Miss CAMPBELL of Jura.

PICKLED HERRINGS.

Herrings	Mace
Pepper and salt	A little butter
1 bay leaf	Vinegar

Take as many herrings as required for pickling. After washing them in cold water and a little salt, remove the heads and tails, split them down the back and take out the backbone; then dry them well in a cloth, sprinkle with a little pepper and salt, and lay on each herring a piece of butter the size of a filbert. Then roll the herring up, beginning at the head, and place in a dish with the bay leaf and mace, and vinegar to cover them; cook in a slow oven for an hour or more.

Miss HUGHES.

PRAWN CREAMS IN ASPIC.

6 oz. prawns	Cress, endive, or parsley
Truffle	About ¾ pint aspic
Pepper	jelly
Salt	A little red colouring
1 gill whipped cream	(carmine)

Dip small tins in cold water, put a little aspic in each, and a tiny piece of truffle to set. (To make aspic jelly liquid, hold basin it is in over hot water). Put 6 oz. of prawns through the mincing machine. Mix them with about ⅜ pint liquid aspic, and just when setting add a gill of whipped cream, salt and pepper and colouring. Before putting the mixture in the tins, pour in a very little more aspic jelly. Allow all to set firm, turn out, surround with chopped aspic jelly, and garnish with cress, endive, or parsley.

Mrs. RODERICK MATHESON,

11 Cresswell Gardens, London, S.W.

RED MULLET.

Butter	1 glass sherry
Flour	Cayenne
½ teaspoonful anchovy sauce	Salt

Clean the fish, take out the gills but leave the inside, fold in oiled paper, bake them gently about 25 minutes. When done take the liquor that flows from the fish, add a thickening of butter kneaded with flour, the anchovy sauce, sherry, cayenne, and salt to taste; let it boil 2 minutes. Serve in a tureen, and let the fish be served either with or without the paper.

BEECHWOOD.

SALMON SOUFFLÉ.

1 lb. of salmon	1 oz. of very thick white sauce
2 oz. of butter	2 eggs
Salt and pepper to taste	

Pound these ingredients (leaving out the whites of eggs) all well together, and rub through a wire sieve. Mix in lightly the whites of the two eggs (which must previously be well beaten). Put into a buttered mould and steam very slowly for about three-quarters of an hour. Serve with a good sauce round it.

Miss CAMPBELL of Jura.

SOLES AUX FINES HERBES.

Soles	Shallots
Butter	Salt and pepper
Parsley	Breadcrumbs

Clean the soles, removing the black skin, scraping the white skin, and wiping well. Put into a fireproof dish large enough to hold the soles some butter the size of an egg. Melt this before a slow fire, then add finely-chopped parsley and shallots and seasoning. Place your soles on the top and cover with parsley, shallot, pepper, salt, and a little melted butter. Pour over them a glass of good white wine, and sprinkle with crumbs of crumbled bread. Then put at various points little pieces of butter, and let it cook on a slow fire. Quarter of an hour before serving put in the oven to colour, and serve in the dish it has been cooked in.

M. P-S., from the French.

SOLES EN POMMES DE TERRE.

Fillets of sole	Seasoning
Some large round potatoes	Fish forcemeat
Cream	White wine
Butter	Fish stock, eggs

Prepare the potatoes for baking, cutting off the top and bottom to make them stand upright. When thoroughly cooked scoop out all the inside (taking great care not to break the skin), pass it through a wire sieve, put it in a stewpan with cream, butter and seasoning, add one yolk of egg. When well mixed and hot line the skins with it, leaving room for the fish, which should be ready cooked.

Take as many fillets as are required, spread them with a fish forcemeat, roll, and cook them in white wine. Put the fillet in the potato, with a little sauce made with fish stock, cream, and yolks of eggs, and cover the top with the potato, using a rose pipe and bag. Put into the oven to brown. The potato for the top is improved by adding a little stiffly-whipped white of egg. Send some sauce separately in a boat.

BELGRAVE SQUARE.

SOLES NORMANDES.

2 soles	Some mushrooms
Butter	2 spoonfuls of flour
White wine	Yolks of 2 eggs
12 oysters	

Take two good soles, remove all skin, and wipe; then place in a long-shaped dish, with butter, wine, oysters, and mushrooms. When cooked take them all out, and make the following sauce:—Melt a piece of butter the size of an egg in a saucepan over a slow fire, then add the flour and mix well with the butter. When the flour has taken a good colour (golden) add half a glass of the liquid in which the fish was cooked, and stir with wooden spoon till your sauce is smooth. When finished add the beaten yolks, and take off the fire. Place your soles finally on a fireproof dish which can go in the oven, and pour over the sauce, placing the mushrooms, etc., round. Put in a warm oven for 15 minutes, and serve.

FRENCH RECIPE.

TO COOK SALT NEWFOUNDLAND FISH.

Keep the salt fish in a dry outside building, if possible. Before cooking, put the quantity required in a pan of tepid water for two days and two nights, changing the water twice a day. Then wash the fish in hot water, and clean away all skin and dark parts and loose bones, and place it, with a little butter rubbed over the fish, in a Dutch oven before a clear fire, and let it slowly cook for an hour to a crisp state and golden colour; then place it in a hot dish, and serve with a little plain butter melted and poured over the fish.

Fish cakes are made with potatoes in the same way as fresh fish cakes, the salt fish being boiled for 20 minutes first, the water to be boiling before putting in the fish.

BEECHWOOD.

TO DRESS FRESH WATER FISH.
(Perch, Dace, Pike, Carp, Tench.)

Butter	Very dry breadcrumbs (grated
½ an onion	from a brown roll or the
3 or 4 washed anchovies	crust of a loaf)

A few spoonfuls good brown sauce

Bone the fish and lay it flat in a fireproof dish, with small pieces of butter under the fish. Chop the onion and anchovies, brown them in a little butter in a small copper saucepan; pour this mixture all along over the fish, strew lightly with the breadcrumbs; add the brown sauce to the dish, and baste the fish in the oven till cooked. Serve in the fireproof dish in which it was cooked.

Col. SANDBACH, Hafodunos.

ADDITIONAL RECIPES.

Kitchen Range Specialists.

JOHN FINLAY & CO., LTD.,

18 Renfield Street, GLASGOW.

FINLAY'S PERFECTION RANGE.
Made in all sizes from 4 feet upwards.

J. F. & CO. HOLD ONE OF THE LARGEST STOCKS OF
KITCHEN AND LAUNDRY FURNISHINGS IN THE
:: :: KINGDOM. :: ::

Write for Catalogue of Prices.

MEATS AND ENTRÉES.

BALLETJE GEHACKT.

1 lb. veal	1 egg
1 slice of bread	Milk and water
Butter, the size of an egg	Seasoning
5 or 6 rusks	Gravy, a *very* little mace

Mince the veal very small, then take a slice of bread the
size of your hand and the rusks and soak them in milk
and water. When well soaked and soft, squeeze as much
of the liquid out of them as possible, add them to the
meat, season with pepper and salt and mace, and blend
them well together with the yolk and white of one egg.
Bake with the butter, pouring some gravy over it from
time to time, and brown it over the top with a salamander.

OLD DUTCH RECIPE from the Hague.

BEEF SOUFFLÉ.

½ lb. lean roast beef	Yolks of 3 and whites of 4
Pepper	eggs
Salt	Shallot

SAUCE.—About 1 oz. butter, ½ tablespoonful flour, 1 tablespoonful mushroom ketchup, a little Worcester or anchovy
sauce, a good teacupful of good beef gravy, pepper and
salt ;—all this to be melted and allowed to thicken.

Mince and pound the beef with the sauce, season it all
well with pepper and salt, and finally add the yolks of
egg. Put through a sieve and mix in some chopped
shallot, and then mix in lightly the stiffly-whipped whites
of egg. Pour all into a soufflé dish, and bake 20 minutes,
laying a paper over the top to prevent it burning.

Mrs. BRODRICK.

TO COOK TOUGH BLACKGAME, etc.

Remove the meat from the breast, leaving the skin. Pound well with a very little butter, put back on the bird, shaping it to the correct shape, cover with the skin and cook as usual.

Mrs. F. BATESON, Bell Farm, Clewer.

TO COOK OLD GAME.

After the customary preparations for cooking, cut off the legs at the knees and the wings at the pinions. Then rub the bird inside and out with about 2 to 4 oz. of butter, according to size of bird. Add a *small* pinch of pepper and salt. Put the bird in a pie dish with plenty of good gravy. Fill up with water. Turn another pie dish over the first. Put the whole into a *slow* oven and stew for 3 hours. Then add a very little gelatine to set the gravy. When quite cold turn the contents of the pie dish on to an ordinary dish, when it will come out as from a mould, in jelly.

Mrs. ROBERT GRAHAM of Skipness.

BOUDINETTES OF COLD MEAT.

Equal quantities of any cold meat and cold potatoes. To each ½ lb. of meat allow 2 teaspoonfuls of chopped parsley, 1 teaspoonful of salt, ½ a teaspoonful of pepper, 1 yolk of egg, stock or milk, breadcrumbs

Chop the meat finely, and if possible put it through a mincing machine. Rub the cold potatoes through a wire sieve. Next add to these ingredients parsley, salt, pepper, and egg in the above proportions. Stir all well over the fire. If too stiff add a little stock or milk. Next smooth the mixture evenly on the plate, and divide it into equal parts, and shape each division into a cone. Brush well over with beaten egg, and then roll in breadcrumbs and fry in fat a golden brown. Drain on kitchen paper, and serve with fresh or fried parsley.

Miss HUGHES.

BRISKET OF BEEF (FRESH).

Brisket of beef	Salt
Butter	Carrot
1 pint good brown stock	Onion
Pepper	Turnip

Trim the beef to a nice shape, bone it and tie it up. Put a piece of butter into the casserole and place it on the stove and make it hot; then put the meat into it, secure the lid and place it on the hot stove. Let it simmer three-quarters of an hour, then add carrot, turnip, onion, salt and pepper to taste; then add the stock, put it on the stove for another hour-and-a-half to finish cooking. Then it is ready for dishing up.

Mrs. Charles Bruce,
13 Chapel Street, London.

CRÊME DE VOLAILLE.

4 oz. chicken or any delicate white meat	Yolks of 2 and whites of 4 eggs ½ pint good cream

Rub the chicken through a sieve, mix in the other ingredients with a spoon, first whipping up the eggs (separately) as for a soufflé; steam in a mould for one hour, add flavouring to taste. A white sauce should be sent round it, with truffles, peas, or plain.

Mrs. Sandbach,
85 Cadogan Gardens, London.

CREAM OF CHICKEN.

4 ounces chicken	Truffles
Whites of 2 eggs	Mushrooms
A little salt	Rich cream sauce
½ pint good cream	

Scrape the chicken and pass it through a very fine sieve, then put it in a mortar and pound well; add the whites of egg, one at a time, and a little salt, and beat well for 10 minutes, then add the cream *slowly*. When all is well mixed pour it into a well-buttered mould or moulds, and steam for 20 minutes. Pour over it rich cream sauce, and garnish with truffles and mushrooms. This is enough for a single entrée only. It can be made of rabbit, or fish also.

Mrs. Charles Kennard, 8 Oxford Square, London.

Historic Cookbooks of the World

Another Recipe.

1 breast of chicken	A little salt
½ oz. pearl barley	1½ pints stock

Cut the chicken into small pieces, put in a stewpan with the stock, barley, and salt. Simmer slowly for 1½ hours, put through sieve and serve.

Mrs. W. E. CRUM.

COLD ENTRÉE.

1 fowl	½ oz. pistachio nuts
1 lb. sausage meat	Pepper and salt
½ lb. ham	1 oz. meat glaze
2 hard boiled eggs	Aspic
Stock	A little grated nutmeg

Bone a fowl, spread half the sausage meat on it, cut the ham in strips, place alternate strips of lean and fat with the hard boiled eggs and pistachio nuts between them, season with pepper and salt and a little grated nutmeg if liked, and spread the remainder of the sausage meat over this. Roll the fowl up tight, place in a cloth and tie the ends securely. Place the stock in a saucepan, and simmer the fowl gently in it for 1½ hours. When nearly cold, loosen the cloth and press between two dishes with a heavy weight on the top. When cold, brush all over with the glaze in a tablespoonful of water, and garnish with aspic.

Miss REED.

JAMAICA WHITE CURRY.

1 cocoanut	2 tablespoonfuls of flour
1 quart cucumber or vegetable marrow, cut in large dice	1½ tablespoonfuls curry powder
	Parsley
	Thyme
1 small onion	2 oz. butter
Some milk	1 Chilli pepper

Put onion and herbs into muslin bag. Grate cocoanut and put it in three pints of boiling water. Put the marrow or cucumber to simmer till tender, with bag of herbs and pinch of salt, just covering it with milk. Just as it boils squeeze the bag of herbs into the saucepan, then take it away. Meanwhile squeeze out in a mortar all the juice of the raw cocoanut, strain it and leave the milky juice to stand; when the cream rises to the top skim it off; do this several times, and get as much cocca-nut cream as you can. Beat the flour and curry powder and butter together in a cup till it is in a paste. Stir it into the saucepan upon the marrow and keep well stirred till it boils. Then boil ten minutes more. Serve with well-boiled rice. Do not let it at any period stick to the saucepan, as it will get brown.

M. P.-S. (Malay Recipe).

INDIAN CURRY.

2 to 6 onions	2 tablespoonfuls of chutney
1 large potato	1 dessert-spoonful curry powder
2 oz. butter (more, if required	(more if liked hot)
richer)	A few drops lemon juice
1 tablespoonful cocoa nut	A little pickle and apple
A little ham or bacon fat	

The vegetables or meat for the curry must be cooked separately.

Peel and slice thin the onions, and cook in a saucepan with the butter till tender and brown, then add the potato raw (cut into dice), which cooks with the onion, grated cocoanut, chutney, curry powder, lemon juice, pickle and apple, ham or bacon fat (which must be passed through a sieve); then add the meat, vegetable, egg, or fish of which the curry is to be made, and serve very hot.

N.B.—Cook the onions 2½ to 3 hours, and each of the other vegetables partly cook before putting them to the onions,—then cook all together till they seem well done. Two onions are generally enough to use.

Mrs. CHAS. BRUCE,

13 Chapel Street, Belgrave Square.

DRY CURRY.

Onions	5 cloves
1 large tablespoonful curry	1 large teacupful of new rich
powder	milk
Butter	5 cardamons
1 lb. fresh mutton or vege-	A small piece of cinnamon
tables	Salt
A little lemon	

Fry some onions a light brown in a large piece of butter, and lay them on a plate. Put into the butter the curry powder, and allow it to fry till it is dry and a dark brown colour, stirring all the time. Then add the mutton and vegetables cut into small dice, and allow to fry until the meat is half-cooked; then add the milk. Pound to a very fine paste the cardamons, cloves, cinnamon, and onions, and mix well into the gravy. When it has thickened, cover the saucepan and allow it to stew until the gravy becomes quite thick. A few minutes before dishing it up, squeeze in a little lemon and add salt. Stir up and serve very hot.

This is an Indian recipe. The sauce made as above and poured over a whole cauliflower previously boiled is a nice luncheon dish, served with rice in another dish.

Mrs. CHARLES BRUCE.

CURRY.

2 or 3 oz. butter	Good strong stock
2 or 3 onions	Salt to taste
⅓ lb. fresh meat	Lemon
1 tablespoonful of curry powder	½ cup of cream
Slice of apple or 2 or 3 gooseberries	

2 or 3 oz. of butter put into a small saucepan until it is quite brown, then 2 or 3 onions cut fine and fry them brown, ⅓ lb. fresh meat cut in pieces, 1 tablespoonful of curry powder mixed over it, put it into the pan and fry until it is a nice brown colour, then add good strong stock and let it stew for about an hour, then add salt, squeeze of lemon, and ½ cup of cream. A slice of apple or 2 or 3 gooseberries improve it.

BALLINLUIG.

CUTLETS À LA RÉFORME.

1 small bottle of truffles	½ lb cooked tongue or
7 eggs	ham

Take the whites of 4 hard boiled eggs, ½ lb. cooked tongue or ham, and 1 small bottle of truffles; cut them in long narrow strips, and put them in a small stew-pan. Mince together the trimmings of the eggs, ham or tongue and truffles; beat up three eggs in a basin with a little salt; dip each cutlet in this, and press an equal quantity of the above mince on both sides of it; dip it again in the egg, breadcrumb it carefully and flatten it with a cutlet bat. Fry in oil on a slow fire about 10 minutes.

SAUCE.—While the cutlets are being fried, melt a piece of butter in a saucepan, add a teaspoonful of flour and stir on the fire until it begins to colour; then add a gill of good stock, 3 cloves, 4 peppercorns, 1 sprig of parsley, 1 of thyme, 1 bay leaf, and a little salt. Let the sauce boil half an hour, skim off the fat, add a wineglassful of sherry, and strain it on the garniture of long, narrow strips mentioned above. Dish up the cutlets in a circle, with the garniture in the centre. Mrs. W. E. CRUM.

FOWL EN CASSEROLE.

Butter
Parsley
Lemon juice

2 oz. clarified dripping
Bunch of herbs
Peppercorn

About a gill stock.

Choose a large and rather old fowl. Truss as for boiling, putting the liver and a piece of butter rubbed up with a little minced parsley and lemon juice inside; put 2 oz. clarified dripping in a casserole with a bunch of herbs (parsley, green onions, bay leaf, etc.) and some peppercorns. Then lay in the fowl and fry it all together, turning it constantly and basting it well till it is a nice golden brown all over. Now pour off most of the fat, add a gill or so of hot stock, bring this to the boil; then draw the pan to the side of the stove, and let it all simmer gently for 1½ hours until the fowl is perfectly tender. Now lift out the bunch of herbs, skim off any extra fat, thicken the sauce if you like, and serve in the sauce in which it was cooked. Mrs. W. E. CRUM.

GALANTINE OR BASSAMORE.

2 lbs. best part of a fillet of veal
½ lb. ham
Yolks of 3 eggs, whites of 2
A little cream

A few breadcrumbs
Pepper, salt, and nutmeg
A little mace
A grated lemon   herbs

Chop all but the eggs and cream very fine, carefully taking out every knot and string from the meat. Mix in the eggs and cream. Boil 1½ hours, tied up in a cloth like a roly-poly pudding; glaze and serve cold.

Mrs. CAMPBELL of Inverneill.

Historic Cookbooks of the World

GAME PIE.

4 to 6 grouse Bacon Seasoning Paste (made of flour and water)	2 lbs. hough of beef Vegetables and herbs A little lard or mutton suet

Take 4 to 6 grouse, according to the size of the dish. Fillet them and thickly lard the fillets. Pick the remainder of the meat off the bones, and pound it with the same quantity of bacon. Season with pepper and salt, place the pounded meat and the larded fillets in alternate layers till the dish is quite full. Cover the dish quite close with the paste, bake in a moderate oven for 1½ hours. Make a good gravy of the bones of the grouse and the hough of beef and vegetables and herbs; it must be a firm jelly. Let the pie stand until cold, pour the gravy over it, and cover with a little lard or mutton suet.

Mrs. GRAHAM of Skipness.

GROUSE SOUFFLÉ.

Cold grouse Two handfuls boiled rice 1 oz. butter	1 tablespoonful meat glaze, dissolved in a little stock Seasoning. 3 eggs

Remove the meat from the bones of the grouse, pound well with the rice, butter, and glaze, season well, and rub all through a wire sieve, then mix in the yolks of the eggs, add the whites, beaten very stiff, steam gently for 1 hour, and serve with brown sauce.

Mrs. ELLISON, The Vicarage, Windsor.

SCOTCH HAGGIS.

Sheep's bag and pluck ¼ lb. minced suet ¼ lb. oatmeal	4 small onions ½ teaspoonful powdered herbs Pepper and salt to taste

Wash bag in cold water, scrape and clean it well, let it lie all night in cold water with salt. Wash the pluck, put it into a pot of boiling water with a tablespoonful of salt. Boil 2 hours, letting the windpipe hang out of pot. When cold, cut off the windpipe, grate half the liver, mince the heart, lights, suet, and onions very small. Add the oatmeal, which has been toasted to a golden brown, the pepper, salt, herbs, and a cupful of the liquor in which the pluck was boiled. Mix well, fill the bag rather more than half with the mixture, and sew it up. Place in a pot of boiling water and boil for three hours, pricking it occasionally to keep it from bursting.

"The Samaritan Cookery Book."

HARE CREAM.

Some cold hare	2 or 3 eggs
Breadcrumbs	Seasoning
Ham	A little milk

Mince the flesh of the hare finely, mixing with it a small quantity of breadcrumbs soaked in milk and squeezed fairly dry, add a savoury seasoning, blend all with two or three eggs, according to the quantity. Well butter a plain mould, fill it with the mixture, cover it with buttered paper, and steam 40 minutes, or a little longer if the cream be a large one. Make a gravy from the bones of the hare, a little thickening and browning, and serve with the cream. Turn out of the mould, and serve with red currant jelly.

Miss REED.

HAM SOUFFLÉ.

1¾ oz. flour	3 eggs
2 oz. butter	1½ wineglassfuls cream
3 drops cochineal	4 tablespoonfuls very finely chopped
A few grains cayenne	cooked ham or tongue
A pinch of salt	Some baked breadcrumbs

Put the flour, 1½ oz. of the butter, cochineal, cayenne, salt, and yolks of eggs in a saucepan, and mix by degrees with the cream. When smooth stir over the fire with a wooden spoon till it boils, add the ham or tongue, the whites of eggs well whipped, mix all lightly together, and pour into a soufflé dish. Sprinkle the top with the breadcrumbs and ½ oz. of butter, cut into small pieces. Bake for half-an-hour in a moderate oven.

Miss CAMPBELL of Jura.

Folklore and Mythology Archive

CROÛTES OF HAM AND BEANS.

4 oz. lean ham
Spoonful of sherry
Cayenne

Purée of broad beans (or white haricot beans)
Croûtes of bread

Grate the ham fine, put in a stewpan with a little cayenne and the sherry. Dish upon small fried croûtes of bread, and put in the centre a purée of beans. Serve hot.

Mrs. CHAS. BRUCE,
13 Chapel Street, London.

HASH.

Put one pint of milk in stewpan with an onion, salt and pepper. Slice your meat and flour it, and put it into the warm milk. Let it simmer for a quarter of an hour and serve.

Mrs. CHAS. BRUCE,
13 Chapel Street, London.

HOT-POT.

2 or 3 lbs. mutton chops
3 lbs. potatoes
Pepper and salt
A sprinkling of curry powder

A little chopped parsley and flour
1 medium-sized onion
2 or 3 mushrooms
2 mutton kidneys

Peel the potatoes. Remove the outside fat from the chops. Place a layer of potatoes at the bottom of a round hot-pot dish, and then a layer of the trimmed chops, then the seasoning and a sprinkling of flour, then kidneys (with the skin removed and cut in halves), then a layer of potatoes and mutton chops, kidneys and mushroom, and more potato at the top. The potatoes at the top to be left whole. Pour over about 1 pink of stock. Bake in a moderate oven from 2½ to 3 hours. Oysters and anchovies are a great improvement.

Miss HUGHES, Beechwood.

HOT-POT.

2½ lbs. rump steak, or mutton chops cut in pieces, 8 or 10 raw potatoes, some small onions and mushrooms, and 6 kidneys.—All put in layers in an earthen pot, seasoned with salt and pepper. Pour over it three or four tablespoonfuls of ketchup, and at the top put two dozen oysters, and, if you have it, a snipe. Cover with a good paste, and bake at least two hours.

Miss STORY, The University, Glasgow.

JUGGED HARE.

A big piece of butter	Some small onions
Some thimblefuls of bacon or fat	Pepper
A spoonful of flour	Salt
Water or thin stock	Bunch of herbs
A little vinegar	Bay leaf
1 glass good red wine	Spices, etc.

When your hare is well cleaned and cut in bits, put into the saucepan the butter and fat, and partly cook the hare till it begins to colour. Take out the hare and put the flour into the sauce to make it thicker, add the water or stock, replace the hare, and add the onions, pepper, salt, herbs, etc., and wine, and allow to cook gently 1½ to 2 hours, according to the size of the hare. Not more than a quarter of an hour before serving remove the hare, and mix a little vinegar with the sauce (this binds it), then pour it over the bits of hare.

Mrs. GRAHAM of Skipness.
(From the French.)

LEG OF MUTTON MARINE.

Salt	Bay leaves
Whole peppers	Half a glass of vinegar
Onions	A bottle or more of red
Shallots	wine
2 cloves	Some sweetened cream

Take a leg of mutton, and pierce it here and there with a knife. Put it in an earthenware dish large enough to turn it in; add salt, whole peppers, sliced onions, shallots, cloves, bay leaves, vinegar and wine. Leave it in the pickle for 2 or 3 days, turning the leg twice a day. Then bake it, basting it with the pickle (of course, larding it with butter or lard before putting it in the oven). When the mutton is roasted, take the gravy from beneath it, add a little sweetened cream and serve it hot. This sauce is called game sauce.

Mrs. GRAHAM of Skipness.
(From the French.)

LIVER PUDDINGS.

| Liver | | Pepper |
| Suet | | Salt |

Boil the liver till tender, then grate it fine. To 1 lb. of liver add ¾ lb. suet. Season with pepper and salt, fill the skins and boil for 20 minutes. They will keep for a fortnight. Boil 15 minutes when required for use.

Mrs. MACDONALD of Dunach.

MEAT PUFFS.

| ½ lb. medium paste (or any | | A little meat |
| trimmings will do for this dish) | | Seasoning |

Roll out the paste as thinly as possible; mince the cold meat very finely, and season. Cut the paste into rounds, wet the edges, cover half of it with the meat, fold the other half over, press and pinch the edges together. Flour, and fry a nice brown, or they may be baked in a quick oven. Miss HUGHES.

MUTTON HAM.

1 good sized bowl of common		1 good sized bowl of
salt		sugar
1 large tablespoonful pepper		1 teaspoonful saltpetre

This is sufficient for two hams. To be rubbed well into the hams; turn every day. Leave for 10 days in the mixture, and then take out and smoke with peat or wood smoke. Mrs. MACDONALD of Dunach.

MUTTON SAUSAGES.

1 lb. underdone leg of mutton		Some sweet herbs
6 oz. beef suet		2 well beaten eggs
1 pint oysters		½ lb. grated bread
2 anchovies		Mace, pepper, and salt

Chop the mutton, suet, oysters, anchovies, and herbs together finely, and season with the mace, pepper, and salt; add the grated bread and well beaten eggs; mix it well and pot it. Use it by rolling into balls the shape of a sausage, and frying them.

Miss L. M'INROY of Lude.

NOISETTES OF MUTTON.

Fillet of mutton		Onion
Salt		Parsley
Coraline pepper		Mushrooms

Take the fillet from a well-hung neck of mutton, and cut into slices ½ inch thick. Bat these out flat and trim in rounds. Season with ingredients as above, and place them in a well buttered saucepan. Fry over a quick fire for 5 minutes. Take them up and mask with sauce as below.

SAUCE.—½ pint good gravy, 1 mushroom, 2 onions, 2 bay leaves, sprig of thyme, a wineglassful of sherry, with 2 raw whites of eggs beaten up, 1 oz. arrowroot, a spoonful of shredded olives.

Mix all but the arrowroot and olives in the order mentioned; simmer 15 minutes, strain, reboil. Add the arrowroot and lastly the olives, and serve after reboiling.

Mrs. W. E. CRUM.

PEPPER POT.

This is a West Indian dish, and may be recommended for sportsmen coming in late. If warmed up every morning and replenished from time to time it will last for years. In some houses in the West Indies there are pepper pots over 100 years old. It is sent to table in the same black earthenware pipkin or "buck pot" in which it is cooked. The following 2 recipes are given by kind permission of the West India Produce Association, 4 Fenchurch Buildings, London, E.C., from whom Cassareep may be obtained.

I.

Cut a loin of young pork into chops. Fry them until brown, and put them with a partially roasted fowl also cut up, with a large onion, a dozen shallots, and a few dry chillies into an earthenware pipkin or "buck pot." Pour over all a sauce consisting of 2 tablespoonfuls of moist cane sugar, 1½ of salt, and a teaspoonful of cayenne pepper, mixed well with hot water, with 7 to 10 tablespoonfuls of cassareep added till brown. Boil, and allow to simmer for $1\frac{1}{4}$ hours. Boil again next day for $\frac{1}{2}$ hour, and on the third day the pepper pot will be ready for table.

II.

Cut some fat fresh pork into dice and fry them brown. Place them with the melted fat in a new pipkin. Add cold meat, fried game, or poultry, cut up, without any vegetables or stuffing, and enough water to cover the meat. To every pint of water add a tablespoonful of cassareep, add chillies or capsicums to taste. The materials should be kept in the pipkin, *and boiled up every morning*. Cold roast meat may be added from time to time. Always be careful to remove the fat on the surface before heating, and invariably serve in the same vessel in which it is cooked. Use only a wooden spoon and fork. Replenish by preparing the meat as above, with a little extra sauce. Cold poultry or game can be put in. Whether used or not the pepper pot must be warmed up every day, and nothing boiled must ever be put in the pot.

PEPPER POT (another Recipe).

2 lbs. ham or bacon	1 tablespoonful sugar
2 lbs. fresh pork	A few dried peppers
1 duck or chicken	A bunch of herbs, tied up in a
(All to be cut up	muslin bag
raw)	2 onions

Half a bottle cassareep, mixed with boiling water.

Put the meat into the liquid, and have the pot almost full, as it goes down considerably. Stew it in the oven for 4 hours, cool, and take off the fat. It is better for being worked two or three days before eating. *Three times a week heat it.* Keep covered when cooking. Do not put gravy into it or fish (but a very good pot can be made in the same way with *only* fish).

All bits of cold meat, fowl, bacon, etc., can be added to it as the contents of the pot get eaten. When cold the contents of the pot should be quite solid.

Mrs. J. E. TINNE,
Mostyn, Aigburth, Liverpool.

PERDRIX AU CHOU.

Partridges	Cabbage
Carrots	Bunch of herbs
Onions	Sausages
Bacon	Nutmeg

A little stock

Lay in the bottom of a saucepan the carrots, onions, herbs, some slices of bacon, sausages, and a cabbage which has been brought to the boil in salted water, well-drained and a little broken; add a little stock and nutmeg. Place the partridges in the middle of the cabbage. If the partridges are old allow them to cook for 5 hours, if young birds 1½ hours. When serving, place the partridges on the bacon and the sausages around.

Mrs. CAMERON, Lochmaben.

PHEASANT IN CASSEROLE.

¼ lb. butter	Salt
½ pint stock	Pepper

Heat the butter and lay the pheasant in it in the casserole. Shut the lid down tight, and let it brown for ¾ of an hour. Add the stock and thicken to taste. Stew for ¾ of an hour. Add salt and pepper to taste and dish up.

Mrs. CHAS. BRUCE.

AN EXCELLENT PIGEON PIE.

6 pigeons	Plovers' eggs
Pepper	Forcemeat
Salt	Calf's head stock
Cayenne	About ¼ wineglassful old
Foiegras	Madeira
Truffles	Lemon juice Paste

Six plump young pigeons, trimmed of all superfluous matter, including pinions and below the thighs. Season with pepper and salt, and stuff with foiegras and quartered truffles, and fill up the pie with *plovers'* eggs and some good forcemeat. Make a good gravy from the superfluous parts of the birds and some calf's head stock, to which has been added the Madeira, lemon juice and cayenne. See that your paste is light and flaky, and bake in a moderate oven for 3 hours. Pour in more gravy just before taking out, and let the pie get cold.

Col. SANDBACH, of Hafodunos.

POTATO POT.

Cover the bottom of a deep dish with potatoes, then mutton chops or beef steak, pepper and salt, and a *little* minced onion, then again potatoes and meat till the dish is full; fill the dish with gravy, and put a *thick* covering of pared potatoes all over the top. A quarter of an hour before taking it out of the oven fill the dish quite up with boiling water.

Mrs. CHARLES BRUCE.

POTATO CUTLETS AUX TOMATES.

Some slices of cold mutton		Salt
Mashed potato		Ripe tomatoes
Pepper		1 or 2 eggs

Spread the potato, nicely flavoured with pepper and salt, on each side of the slices of mutton. Then take the tomatoes, remove their skins by plunging them into hot water, stew them in a large saucepan, and break into them one or two eggs (one egg to four large tomatoes), stirring the mixture well round until it is of the consistency of scrambled egg. Pile up the tomatoes in centre of dish, arranging cutlets, which should be fried to a light golden brown colour, round the tomatoes, which should be bright pink Purée of other vegetables can be used instead of the tomatoes.

Mrs. W. E. CRUM.

TO PICKLE BEEF.

4 gallons water		2 oz. saltpetre
1¼ lbs. brown sugar		8 lbs. salt

It is a great improvement to add ¼ oz. allspice, ¼ oz. pepper, and 20 cloves.

Boil the water, sugar, saltpetre, and salt (and spices, if liked) in a pot carefully, taking off the scum as it rises; when no more scum rises let it boil 20 minutes longer, then take it off, and let it stand till cold. When quite cold, cover the meat completely with it. Boil the pickle up every month, skim it carefully, and add a couple of handfuls of common salt. In this way it will keep for months. For tongues, put ½ lb. saltpetre into the same mixture.

Always rub the meat with a little salt, and let it draw a few hours before putting it into the pickle. Keep the meat closely covered.

This quantity of pickle is for a very large quantity of meat; it never becomes too salt.

The tongues, after having been in pickle from a month to six weeks, may be dried and hung in paper bags.

Mrs. CAMPBELL of Inverneill.

PRESSED BEEF (pickling for 8 lbs. Beef).

2 lbs. of common salt	A little black pepper
½ lb. coarse sugar	½ oz. of allspice
¼ oz. pounded saltpetre	4 or 5 bay leaves

Take a piece of the thick flat rib, rub the sugar well into the beef and let it stand 6 hours; then shake a little black pepper over the meat, and let it stand 3 hours, and then rub in the salt. Turn it daily in the liquor for 10 days, soak in water for a few hours, and then put it into a pan, cover with cold water, bring it to the boil, and take off the scum. Put in ½ oz. of allspice and 4 or 5 bay leaves, and cook gently about 3½ hours.

Miss HUGHES.

PRESSED BEEF.

| 12 lbs. brisket | 2 oz. saltpetre |
| ¼ lb. juniper berries | 2 oz. bay salt. |

Cut the brisket from the thick, not too fat. Bone it, and lay in cold water for 12 hours. Take out and lay in a pan or deep dish with the other ingredients, let it remain in two nights. Then put the beef into pickle, made as below, for 10 days (that exact time is necessary for the proper colouring). Boil for 4 hours.

PICKLE.—3 gallons water, 6 lbs. salt, 1 lb. moist sugar, ½ lb. juniper berries, boiled for 15 minutes. The juniper can be got at a chemist's. BEECHWOOD.

QUENELLES.

Equal quantities of meat, breadcrumbs soaked in milk and butter	A little seasoning
	A little cream
	A well-beaten egg

Pound well in a mortar the meat, breadcrumbs, and butter, add the other ingredients, and mix to a firm paste.

Pound all well again, pass through a fine sieve, and poach for about 10 minutes.

ANOTHER RECIPE.—Pound well ½ lb. veal, rabbit or chicken, and rub through a wire sieve. Mix in with a spoon gradually about ½ pint well-beaten cream, add a little salt, shape with a large spoon, or put in moulds, poach in pan of hot water, and steam for 10 minutes.

Macaroni Quenelles.

Line small plain upright moulds with boiled macaroni, coiling it carefully to touch itself all the way up; fill with quenelle mixture, and poach as for quenelles. Turn out, and place a small mushroom or bit of truffle, etc., on the top of each quenelle.

Mrs. F. BATESON, Bell Farm, Clewer.

SAUTÉ RABBIT.

Take as much flesh off the rabbit as possible, removing the thin skin, also take the legs. Melt 1 oz. of butter in a saucepan, when melted, drop in the rabbit and stir. Sprinkle with salt, pepper, and flour, and after about 5 or 10 minutes add a *small* quantity of hot water. Put cover on saucepan, and leave to simmer for about an hour, stirring occasionally.

Mrs. W. E. CRUM.

RAVIOLI.

Pastry
2 oz. of white chicken, roasted
1 oz. of ham
4 anchovies

A handful of cooked spinach
¼ lb. of cheese
The yolks and whites of 2 raw eggs
Salt and pepper to taste

1 oz. of Parmesan cheese

Wash the anchovies and mince them finely with the chicken, ham, and spinach; season with pepper and salt. Squeeze all moisture from the cheese, add it to the mixture with the Parmesan cheese; pound all together, stir into this the yolks of the eggs, with the whites whipped to a froth. Divide this forcemeat into small portions, and fold each in thin paste and shape like a tiny cutlet or rissole. Put them into fast boiling stock or water for 5 minutes, then take them out, and sprinkle Parmesan cheese over the top ones, and brown the whole in a shallow pan in the oven.

Mrs. PLOWDEN of Strachur.

JAMES SNEDDON & Co

Glass & China Merchants,

25=31 QUEEN STREET,

GLASGOW.

Dinner Sets.   Tea Sets.

Dessert Sets.

Toilet Sets.   Vases, &c., &c.

TRADE SUPPLIED.

ONLY ADDRESS:

25-31 QUEEN STREET.

RISOTTO ALLA MILANESE.

1 onion	2 teacupfuls rice
5 oz. butter	3 or 4 threads saffron
2 quarts meat or fish stock	1 tablespoonful grated Parmesan cheese

Cut the onion in slices, fry it in 4 oz. butter, after a few minutes add 1 tablespoonful stock, take away onion, add rice and saffron, mix well with the butter, add by degrees the stock, letting the rice cook over a very hot fire. When the rice is quite soft and has absorbed all the liquor, add the cheese and stir in an ounce of butter.

Miss STORY, The University, Glasgow.

RABBIT À LA CHASSEUR.

1 rabbit	1 tumblerful of claret
	Bacon and onions

Cut a rabbit into neat joints, fry it in a pan with square pieces of bacon and onion. After it is fried pour in the claret and stew till tender.

Mrs. CAMPBELL of Inverneill.

ROMAN PUDDING.

1 nice rabbit	½ pint cream or good milk
2 oz. of cheese	Good paste
1 small shallot	Good brown sauce
Pepper and salt to taste	

Boil the rabbit, take off the meat and cut into small pieces, or mince it. Grate the cheese and chop the shallot very fine; add the cream, pepper and salt, and mix well together. Line a buttered tin with paste, fill with the mixture, and bake for one hour. Serve with good brown sauce. Veal or fowl may be used in the same way, with a sprinkling of mace.

Miss REED, Horsham.

SAVOURY PIE.

1½ lbs. rump of beef	A little flour and butter
1 quart water	2 tablespoonfuls vinegar
1 onion 1 clove	Potatoes
A small bit of mace	Egg and forcemeat balls

Cut the beef in pieces about the size of a walnut, put in a jar with water (cold); add the onion, clove, and mace. Stew well, pour off the gravy, and thicken it with the flour and butter ; add the vinegar (hot). Before serving, put in the force meatballs and potato, the latter cut about the size of a lump of sugar. This looks best served in a raised ornamental pie-dish.

Mrs. CAMPBELL of Inverneill.

SCOTCH COLLOPS.

2 lbs. tender side of a round of beef
Pepper and salt

1 slice of loaf grated ⎫
1 apple minced   ⎬ mixed
1 small onion minced ⎭

Beat the beef with a rolling pin, then cut it in pieces. Rub the saucepan with beef suet, put a layer of the beef in the bottom, shake the bread, apple, and onion over it, and pepper and salt ; then put another layer of beef, and so on till finished. Cover with a lid and cook very slowly till ready.

Miss L. M'INROY of Lude.

SHEEP'S HEAD.

1 sheep's head
2 tablespoonfuls pearl barley (or rice)
2 onions
2 small carrots
1 small turnip

Parsley
Thyme
Bay leaf
10 Peppercorns
Salt
Pepper

Cut the head in half, remove the brains, wash them and put into cold water with a little salt. Wash the head in several waters, carefully remove any splintered bones, and let it soak in salt and water for an hour. Cover with cold water, bring to the boil, pour away the water, replace with fresh cold water, add parsley, etc., peppercorns and salt; boil up and skim well. The head must be cooked slowly for about 3 hours; $1\frac{1}{2}$ hours before serving add the vegetables (sliced), with the rice or barley.

SAUCE.—$1\frac{1}{2}$ oz. butter, $1\frac{1}{2}$ oz. flour, brains, seasoning. Remove skin and fibre from the brains, tie them in muslin, boil for 10 to 15 minutes in the liquor that the head was cooked in, then chop them coarsely. Heat the butter in a stewpan, add flour, stir over the fire for 2 or 3 minutes, then add $\frac{3}{4}$ pint liquor from the pot, simmer for 10 minutes, add brains, season to taste, and keep hot till required.

Miss STORY, The University, Glasgow.

SHEEP'S HEAD MOULD.

A good-sized head, plotted if possible, if not skinned	Hard-boiled egg Pepper and salt

Boil the head till the meat leaves the bones easily, then take it off the fire and leave it till cold. Boil down the liquid to a pint, cut the head up in small bits, slice the tongue, line the bottom of a bowl with hard-boiled egg, then a layer of meat, season well with black pepper and salt, and as you fill up pour the liquid over. Leave it standing in a cool place all night, and it should then turn out very firm.

Miss L. M'Inroy of Lude.

SHEEP'S HEAD PIE.

A sheep's head Ham or bacon (cooked)	2 or 3 eggs (hard-boiled) Pepper, salt, and mixed spice

Wash the head thoroughly, and boil till the bones shake out, strain the stock from the head, and cut slices of the ham or bacon. Cut the head in small pieces and put layers of it and the ham alternately into a pie dish, with the eggs (cut in slices), and season with the pepper, salt, and spices. Pour in the stock of head, and cover with a paste, and bake $\frac{3}{4}$ of an hour.

Miss L. M'Inroy of Lude.

SNIPE PUDDING.

6 fresh snipe Cayenne Lemon juice 1 onion 1 tablespoonful flour Chopped mushrooms	Parsley A suspicion of garlic Nutmeg Herbs Truffles Suet Paste ½ pint wine

Halve the snipe, removing the gizzards and reserving the trail. Season the snipe with cayenne and lemon juice, and set aside till required. Slice up the onion, fry a light brown colour, add the mushrooms, parsley, garlic, nutmeg and herbs; moisten with wine and boil all for 10 minutes, then add the trail and rub through a sieve. Line a basin with suet paste rolled thin, put in the snipe, the sauce and some truffles; cover the top with paste, steam $1\frac{1}{2}$ hours, and serve hot.

Miss Walder, Horsham.

STEWED STEAK WITH CHESTNUTS.

A piece of tender steak	Pepper, salt
A little good gravy	Chestnuts (peeled and scraped)

Half fry the steak in dripping, then flour it lightly and put in a stewpan with the gravy, season with pepper and salt, let it simmer a few minutes, add the chestnuts, and stew all together until the chestnuts are quite tender.

Mrs. BRODRICK, Liverpool.

SPICED ROUND BEEF.

20 lbs. beef	½ oz. mace
¼ lb. bay salt	1½ lbs. common salt
3 oz. saltpetre	1 lb. suet
¼ oz. cloves	As much water as will cover the beef

Pound finely and mix together the salt, saltpetre, cloves, mace, and bay salt; rub them on the beef; turn it in this pickle every day for a fortnight, and rub it with the liquor. To cook it, put it in a pot with as much water as will cover it, after having first wrapped it round with a tape, and placed the chopped suet on top; then tie a paper over the pot to keep in the steam; bake it 8 hours. Let it remain in the liquor till cold, first tightening the tape. Sometimes it is left two days in the liquor before being used. Mrs. CAMPBELL of Inverneill.

STEWED OX CHEEKS.

Ox cheeks	Sugar
Onions	Seasoning

Steep half-an-hour in salt and water. Wash through five or six waters (as washing cloths). Brown in the pan with onions and a little sugar. Cover with boiling water. Let it stand five hours, *simmering very gently*. Reduce gravy and dish up, served with glazed onions.

Reducing gravy is best done by placing the pan, with lid on, for say the last of the five hours, *in the oven*. Of course, pepper and salt to taste.

Miss STIRLING, Gargunnock, Stirling.

STUFFED PLOVERS or any Small Birds.

Take as many birds as required, bone the birds, stuff with the stuffing as below, fasten each bird with a band of buttered paper, put a piece of fat bacon on the breast of each, place them in a greased pan, and put them into a moderate oven for 20 minutes to half-an-hour. Then take out the birds, remove the paper, and place them on a shallow dish to get cold. When cold, mask them over with aspic jelly. Trim, and dish each with fancy paper, and garnish with watercress or parsley. Serve as a lunch or supper dish.

LIVER STUFFING FOR BIRDS.—Cut into small pieces 8 ozs. of game or poultry livers, 4 ozs. of fat bacon, 4 ozs. of chicken or rabbit, and half a small onion. Put all together in a saucepan, with 1 oz. of butter or any fat, 2 bay leaves, a sprig of parsley, pepper and salt. Fry for five minutes, and pound while hot in a mortar, and rub through a wire sieve. Mix the purée with 1 raw yolk of egg, 2 or 3 chopped mushrooms, an ounce of paté de foie gras if at hand, pepper and salt.

Miss HUGHES.

SWEETBREADS LARDED.

2 sweetbreads	A bunch of sweet herbs
Bacon	Spices and seasoning to taste
Onions	A small quantity rich stock
Carrots	

Trim the sweetbreads, soak them half-an-hour in tepid water, then parboil for a few minutes, and lay them in cold water; when quite cold take out and dry them, lard them thickly with fine strips of bacon; put a slice of fat bacon in a stewpan with the stock, vegetables, etc., lay the sweetbreads on this, stew gently till quite done, basting the top occasionally with the liquor. When cooked strain the liquor, skim off the fat, and reduce the former to a glaze. Brown the larded side of the sweetbreads with a salamander, and serve with sauce over them.

Mrs. W. E. CRUM.

CUTLETS OF SWEETBREADS.

| 1 or 2 calves' sweetbreads | Vegetables for centre |
| Eggs and crumbs | Sauce |

Soak the sweetbreads in warm salted water for 2 hours, parboil them, trim, and simmer for 10 minutes, place

them between two plates and press till cold. Then cut
in slices half-an-inch thick, dry in a little flour, egg and
crumb them, and fry them in a bath of fat. Serve round
a centre of peas, cucumber or macédoine of vegetables,
with good brown or other carefully and lightly-flavoured
sauce. Mrs. BRODRICK, Liverpool.

TO DO UP TURKEY OR CHICKEN.

Stock		Burnt sugar
1 onion		Pepper
Turnips		Salt

Take the wing bones and a portion of the legs or anything that is left, and divide into reasonable-sized pieces.
Take some cold stock that has been well flavoured with
vegetables, add a little more onion, chopped fine. Stew
by the side of the stove till the meat is tender, not broken
away. Add a good quantity of turnips cut into dice, and
a small amount of burnt sugar, pepper and salt. Stew
all together till the turnips are cooked and the stock
reduced. Serve in a hash dish.

Mrs. CHAS. BRUCE.

A PRETTY COLD ENTRÉE.

Parsley		Aspic
Tomatoes		Cress
Rich white mince		

Halve some rather large tomatoes (or small ones with the
stalk side cut off are perhaps better, but then double as
many are required), scoop out a little of the pulp, and
replace with the mince, piled rather high and decorated
with chopped parsley. Dish round a centre of chopped
aspic and mustard and cress.

LITTLE VEGETABLE BOXES.

Take some carrots and turnips, cut them the shape of a
little box, take off a slice for a lid, scoop out the inside;
boil them, when cooked fill with highly-seasoned mince
or minced curry. Serve with rich brown or curry sauce,
but they are quite as nice without sauce.

Mrs. W. E. CRUM.

VEAL CUTLETS À LA BORDELAISE.

Veal cutlets		Pepper
Egg		Shallots
Breadcrumbs		Parsley
Salt		

Trim the cutlets, season with salt and pepper, cover with a light stuffing of shallots, minced parsley, salt and pepper, and dip in egg and breadcrumbs. Butter a stewpan and allow the cutlets to cook slowly in it; when done arrange them in a ring on a plate, and pour a Sauce Bordelaise into the centre.

SAUCE BORDELAISE.

5 or 6 shallots		2 or 3 spoonfuls olive oil
1 onion		A glass of wine
Garlic		Salt
Marrow		Pepper

Mince the shallots, the onion and garlic, allow them to cook very slowly for some minutes in the olive oil, add the Bordeaux, salt, pepper, and allow to cook more quickly until reduced by half, then add a little marrow, already melted. Mix the sauce with a wooden spoon, and when it comes to the boil draw the pan to a cooler part, and allow to cook slowly for a quarter of an hour Serve very hot.

Mrs. CAMERON, Lochmaben.

VEAL OLIVES.

Some slices of veal		1 shallot
Some slices of fat bacon		Cayenne pepper
Egg		Mushrooms
About ½-pint brown gravy		Egg balls
Forcemeat		

Cut the veal in thin rather wide slices, from 3 to 4 inches long, lay on each slice a very thin slice of bacon, then a layer of forcemeat, a little shallot sliced as thin as possible, with pepper, salt, and cayenne. Roll them round, and fasten each securely with a small skewer. Brush them over with egg, fry a nice brown, and pour round the mushrooms boiled in the gravy. Garnish with egg balls.

Miss REED, Wimblehurst, Horsham.

BARLEY CREAM.

1 lb. veal cutlet	Salt to taste
Tablespoonful of pearl barley	1 pint cold water
	1 or 2 tablespoonfuls of cream

Remove skin and fat from the veal, cut it up very finely, put into a pan with the pearl barley, salt, and cold water, boil slowly 3 hours, strain off all the liquid and put it on one side. Put the barley and veal in a mortar and thoroughly pound it. Rub it through a wire sieve, moisten with the liquid, which is all to be added to it. Pour it into a saucepan to warm up, pepper and salt may be added to taste. Stir it up well. One or two table-spoonfuls of cream may be added when used, but only as it is used or it will not keep.

Mrs. W. E. CRUM.

HASTY PUDDING.

3 oz. oatmeal	1½ oz. suet, chopped
1 onion, chopped	Parsley

Fry the suet till brown, then add the onion and parsley. Toss in frying-pan for 20 minutes till brown, then stand the frying-pan aside to simmer slowly till the onions are cooked, then add the oatmeal and serve very hot. Or the skins may be filled with this mixture before cooking, or it may be made without onions or parsley.

Miss ELLEN McINTYRE,
62 Ridgmount Gardens, London, W.C.

BLACK PUDDING.

6 oz. sheep's blood	1 oz. garlic
2 oz. suet	1½ oz. bitter almonds

Put the blood in a clean pan or basin, add the suet and garlic, stir well till all is mixed, and add the almonds, chopped very fine. The skins should be filled with a large funnel.

Miss E. McINTYRE,
62 Ridgmount Gardens, London, W.C.

PORK PIE PASTE (Hot).

2 lbs. soft flour	2 oz. butter
8 oz. lard	Half-pint water, ½ oz. salt

Put water in saucepan with lard and butter and salt ; put flour in a basin, and when the water boils (be sure that it does boil) pour over the flour and mix at once with a large spoon.   Make up into a firm paste, cover it up with a cloth till cool enough, then block on your pie mould, using plenty of flour, or, better still, rice flour, to keep your paste from sticking to the mould.   When well set fill with your chopped pork.   Stamp your lids out with a proper-sized cutter, damp with wet brush, then pinch lid on tight, make two small holes in lid, brush over with egg, and bake in good sound oven (if too cool the pies will drop in the oven).   For 1 lb. pies bake about 1 hour ; when the gravy that boils out of the pies through the holes browns they will be done.

For 1 lb. weight pies use 10 oz. of paste and 8 oz. seasoned meat.   While hot from the oven fill up with gravy or gelatine through the hole in lid with a small funnel.

Mr. THOMAS HILL.

ADDITIONAL RECIPES.

ADDITIONAL RECIPES.

Folklore and Mythology Archive

VEGETABLES.

BEETROOT SALAD.

The yolk of a hard-boiled egg, well bruised, with a little salt and a small spoonful of mustard, then add a table-spoonful of cream, 2 of milk, and 1¼ of vinegar.

This salad is made of beetroot, boiled, sliced rather thick, some celery and, if approved, a small onion, well boiled and pulled in pieces; add the white of an egg as garnish.

Mrs. CAMPBELL of Inverneill.

FRIED BEETROOT.

½ a boiled beetroot	A sprinkling of flour
2 ozs. butter	A little parsley
½ of onion	Salt
¼ clove of garlic	Pepper
1 dessertspoonful of vinegar	

Cut the beetroot into slices and place with the other ingredients (the onion and parsley chopped fine) in a frying-pan. Let them simmer 10 minutes or quarter of an hour, and serve.

Miss STORY.

DRESSED CABBAGE.

1 nice green cabbage	2 tablespoonfuls good stock
1 onion	2 tablespoonfuls of cream
Yolk of 1 egg	

Boil the cabbage, fry the onion and pass it through a wire sieve with the cabbage; add the stock and cream, and yolk, and heat in a stewpan. It looks like spinach.

Mrs. W. E. CRUM.

PURÉE OF CARROTS.

Carrots	Weak stock or water
Onion	Sugar
Celery	Salt
Turnip	Cream

Get some nice red carrots, slice them thin, add an onion also sliced, a little celery and a turnip. Braize all together in some weak stock or water till quite tender. Pass the whole through a tammy or hair sieve. About an hour before serving place it in a stewpan over the fire, and let it simmer gently to clarify. Season with sugar and salt, and work in a little cream just before serving.

Mrs. CHAS. BRUCE.

CHAMPIGNONS À LA MOELLE.

Mushrooms	Shallot
Pepper	1 oz. butter
Salt	½ oz. glaze
Parsley	1 tablespoonful sherry or
4 tablespoonfuls good brown	mushroom liquor
stock	Beef marrow

Peel some nice clean fresh mushrooms, about 2 inches in diameter, season with pepper and salt, chopped parsley and a very small portion of shallot. Put them in a well-buttered saucepan with 1 tablespoonful of the stock, and a small piece of butter on each, cover with buttered paper, and cook in a moderately hot oven for 15 minutes. Put the rest of the stock, the glaze, sherry (or mushroom liquor), and half a shallot into a small stewpan and let it boil up. Having blanched the marrow, cut it in slices about half-an-inch thick, and cook in the sauce until tender; the sauce must not boil after the marrow is added, or it will melt and spoil.

Place each mushroom on a round of buttered toast its own size on a very hot dish, pour over them the sauce, and place a slice of marrow on each. This dish must be served very hot.

Miss HUGHES.

CHESTNUTS AU JUS.

Chestnuts	A few spoonfuls very good
2 tablespoonfuls sugar	strong glaze
1 oz. butter	

Remove the outer skin, and throw the chestnuts into boiling water to enable you to remove the inner skin; then lay them in cold water while the following mixture is prepared:—Stir the sugar and butter in a saucepan till the sugar is browned, let it boil up and add a little cold water; put in the chestnuts, simmer till tender, but do not shake them (to avoid crumbling). Just before serving add a few spoonfuls of glaze.

Mrs. CHARLES BRUCE.

FRENCH BEANS (for 3 or 4 persons).

1 lb. green French beans	Pepper
Butter, the size of an egg	Parsley
Salt	

Pick and wash the beans, place to cook in boiling water with a little salt. Do not cover them during the cooking, that they may remain green. When the water begins to boil you must count 15 or 20 minutes to allow them to cook; take up and put in a strainer. Put a saucepan on the fire with the butter; when melted put in your beans and shake about, powder with chopped parsley, salt and pepper, and serve hot.

FRENCH RECIPE.

GNOCCHI ALLA ROMANA.

1 quart milk	Yolk of 1 egg
1½ oz. butter	Handful grated Parmesan cheese
3 oz. semolina	Pepper and salt to taste

Pour a quart of milk (less one third of a glass, which please keep), into a deep saucepan, add 1½ oz. of butter, pepper and salt to taste, place over the fire and stir to prevent milk from burning until milk comes to the boil, then place the saucepan on the side of the fire and gradually drop into the milk (stirring quickly) 3 oz. of semolina, cook for 10 minutes, then remove from the fire again and mix with this the remaining one-third of the glass of milk, in which you have mixed 1 yolk of egg. Go on mixing carefully near the fire, but without boiling, to get the mixture like velvet, then add a handful of grated Parmesan cheese, and pour, when smooth, the whole mixture on to a marble slab or wooden board, lightly wetted with water, smooth it out to the thickness of half an inch, and then let it cool for 2 hours. When the mixture is cold and well thickened, cut it into pointed dice an inch wide, which place symmetrically in a shallow pan which previously has been well buttered, strew over each layer some grated Parmesan cheese and some drops of liquefied butter. Quarter of an hour before lunch place the Gnocchi in the oven and bake to a golden brown. Sometimes add to the cheese a *little* nutmeg.

Mrs. PLOWDEN of Strachur.

Old Recipe for Cooking a Vegetable Marrow.

A ripe marrow, to every pound of fruit allow 1 lb. refined sugar and 1 lemon, gingerine to flavour.

Peel and core the marrow, cut it into good-sized dice; boil the suger to a syrup, with the rind and juice of the lemon in it. When the syrup is ready put the pieces of marrow in, and boil *slowly* till they are transparently clear. Season with gingerine, which is *very* strong.

Mrs. OMOND.

VEGETABLE MARROW.

| Marrow | Butter |
| Toast | Sweet chutney |

Peel a young vegetable marrow, cut it across in slices the thickness of a finger, and put them in a tin in a moderate oven, with a little piece of butter on each. Bake for nearly an hour. Prepare some pieces of toast, slightly buttered and hot. Lay a slice of the vegetable marrow on each piece. Warm in butter a little of the sweet chutney, put half a teaspoonful of it on each and serve.

Mrs. CHARLES BRUCE.

CURRIED LENTILS (Chinese Dish).

1 breakfast-cupful of pink lentils (Egyptian)	1 teaspoonful best curry powder
3 oz. butter	A clove of garlic (or small onion chopped small)
1 teaspoonful vinegar	Boiled rice
1 small saltspoonful salt	

Soak the lentils overnight in cold water. Next day boil in just enough water to cover them, adding the butter, vinegar, and salt. Stir all constantly to prevent burning on to the pan. When all the water is absorbed and the lentils reduced to a smooth paste, add the curry powder and onion (which has been fried in butter till a good brown). Make all very hot, pile in the centre of a dish, and place a good border of boiled rice round it.

Miss CAMPBELL of Jura.

MUSHROOMS À LA CREME.

½ pint mushrooms	Pepper
½ pint good stock	Salt
½ oz. flour	Powdered mace
½ oz. butter	Parsley
¼ pint good cream	Bread

Remove stalks and skins from mushrooms, sprinkle with seasoning. Heat the stock, put in the mushrooms, bring to the boil and simmer for quarter of an hour. Take out the mushrooms and keep them hot. Add to the stock the butter, kneaded with the flour, stir till thick over the fire, add the cream, stir till nearly boiling, and pour this sauce over the mushrooms. Serve with fried bread and parsley.

Mrs. GEDDES, St. John's Manse, Largs.

PEAS WITH SUGAR.

Shell and wash your peas, put in a saucepan with a piece of butter the size of an egg, 3 or 4 onions, a piece of parsley and thyme, a lettuce heart, a piece of sugar the size of a walnut, and a pinch of salt. Cover your saucepan with a soup-plate, into which you put ½ glassful of water, and fill up by degrees as the water dries. Shake the peas from time to time, and cook on slow fire for an hour. Take out and serve.

From the French.

POMMES DE TERRE À LA CREME.

Dish of potatoes	Tablespoonful flour
1 oz. butter	Salt, pepper, parsley to taste
	Wineglass cream

Having washed and pared the potatoes in salt and water, cut them into slices. Make a sauce in the saucepan (or stewpan) of the butter, flour, **salt**, pepper, parsley, and cream (in the order mentioned), stir till it boils, then pop the potatoes into the sauce. *Serve very hot.* (Eschalots, well chopped, may be added if liked, also grated nutmeg.)

BEECHWOOD.

BALLOON POTATOES.

Cut the potatoes in slices about a quarter of an inch thick. Put a pan with fat on the fire. As soon as the fat is melted, put in the potatoes and let them cook. When they begin to rise to the top they are ready to take out in the cage. Lay them aside till the fat is *very* hot, *steaming*. Then put the cage with the already nearly cooked potatoes into it for a minute. They burst out into a balloon. Kidney potatoes are the best.

Mrs. W. E. CRUM, Fyfield.

German way of Warming up Potatoes.

Boil them, let them get cold, cut them into thin slices into a fireproof dish, add a little butter and milk, grate some Parmesan cheese on the top, and bake in the oven.

Mrs. CHARLES BRUCE.

SOUFFLÉ POTATOES.

12 medium-sized potatoes	Salt
3 whites of egg	½ gill cream (or cream and
2 oz. butter	milk)

Roast the potatoes, cut out a piece of skin at the top about the size of a shilling, scoop out all the insides and do them up with butter, salt and cream, making it very light. Then whip up the whites of egg to a snow and add it to the potato. Put all into a saucepan, warm up, fill the skins with the mixture and then place them in the oven for about 10 minutes, till it rises at the top of the potato.

Mrs. CAMPBELL of Inverneill.

NEW POTATOES.

About a tablespoonful of butter or dripping		Some new potatoes all the same size
	Salt	

Wash and scrape the potatoes, then wipe dry. Warm the butter in a stewpan, lay the potatoes in (they must not be one on the top of the other), allow them to cook very slowly for three-quarters of an hour; when half done add a little fine salt.

Mrs. CAMERON,
National Bank House, Lochmaben.

POTATO SALAD.

Boil some little German potatoes till the skin comes off; when cold, cut them into neat slices and arrange in a dish.

Mix 2 tablespoonfuls of salad oil, 1 dessert-spoonful of vinegar, salt and pepper to taste. Beat till as thick as cream, then pour over potatoes, and sprinkle some finely-chopped parsley over the top. Sliced gherkins may be added.   Mrs. BEVAN.

MASHED POTATOES.

To every lb. of potatoes 1 oz of butter and 2 tablespoonfuls of milk

Boil the potatoes in the usual way. Put the butter and milk in a basin, and place it on the side of the stove to get hot. Take the potatoes when nice and dry and press them through a wire sieve into the basin with the butter and milk; beat well with a wooden spoon for a few minutes, and serve at once.

Miss HUGHES.

RICE FOR CURRY.

Put your rice into boiling water with a little salt. Boil very fast for 15 or 20 minutes, not longer. Pour it into a sieve, wash it well under the cold water tap, then put it in front of a bright fire to dry or on the rack over the kitchen range, turn it about with a wooden spoon so as to dry it. Drop a few drops of lemon juice into the rice when boiling, it whitens and sweetens it.

Mrs. CHARLES BRUCE.

RIZ À LA GRECQUE.

1 onion	1 pint tomato juice
1 pint broth or good stock	1 lb. Patna rice
¼ lb. butter	Pepper

Chop an onion very fine and fry in fresh butter till of a nice brown colour, and then add to it the tomato juice, which has previously passed through a hair sieve, and add also the broth or stock. Place upon the fire, and when boiling add to it the (well-washed) Patna rice, and let it boil until the rice has absorbed the whole of the liquor. Add ¼ lb of butter to it. Put the saucepan in the oven for a quarter of an hour or 20 minutes, stirring the rice occasionally with a fork. When dishing it up, sprinkle over it a pinch of pepper.

Mrs. W. E. CRUM.

SALAD.

Put 1 saltspoonful of salt and 1 of pepper in the bottom of the bowl, mix it well with 1 tablespoonful of the best oil you can get (the quality of the oil is very important), then add 1 tablespoonful of Tarragon vinegar (in preference to common vinegar), and stir it well, then add three more spoonfuls of oil and mix well, then *break* your lettuces into it (they should be quite dry), and add any other stuff such as beetroot, celery, etc. Mix it all up at the moment of serving.
G. R. P.

SALSIFY.

Salsify	A little cream and anchovy
Butter	sauce
Breadcrumbs	Pepper (or pepper wine)

Wash the salsify well and boil for 1½ hours, then scrape it and cut it in pieces the size of oysters. Butter some shells and breadcrumb them, then lay the salsify in the shells in the same way as you would oysters, pour the cream and anchovy sauce on the top, then strew over them bread-crumbs and pieces of butter, brown for 10 or 12 minutes in the oven. Serve very hot, A little pepper or pepper wine is an improvement. Ramakin cases are suitable instead of shells.

Mrs. SAM. SANDBACH of Cherryhill.

SAVOURY RICE CROQUETTES.

A handful of rice		Parsley
Water		Pepper and salt
Butter		Egg and breadcrumbs
Parmesan cheese		(Ham)

Boil the rice in just as much water as the rice will absorb when done whole (without being too wet). When the rice has sucked up all the water, stir in a small piece of butter and some grated Parmesan cheese; add pepper and salt to taste, and spread out the rice on a plate; when cold make it into the shape of croquettes, and egg and breadcrumb them. Fry in hot lard and serve with hot parsley. Put if you like a little grated ham instead of or as well as the cheese.

Mrs. W. E. CRUM.

TOMATO AND APPLE SALAD.

4 large tomatoes		1 large apple
	1 teaspoonful Spanish onion	

Take 4 large tomatoes, dip them into boiling water, and remove the skins; slice about a quarter of an inch thick, and then cut into dice. Chop finely a teaspoonful of Spanish onion, or a couple of chives, and mix them with 1 large peeled, cored, and chopped apple. Mix together lightly, and pour over any good dressing. Do not chop or add the apple till just before it is required.

Miss HUGHES.

PURÉE OF TURNIPS.

Turnips		Butter
¼ lb. rice		Pepper
Milk to taste		Salt

Wash and skin the turnips, cut them into very small pieces, cook them in water with half-a-pound of rice, a piece of butter, pepper and salt. When cooked, pass through a sieve, mix with milk to taste, and serve.

Mrs. CAMERON, Lochmaben.

WALDORF SALAD.

| 3 good eating apples | 2 teaspoonfuls of powdered |
| 2 heads of celery | sugar |

A good stiff Mayonnaise dressing

Chop fine the apples and celery, and add the sugar. Mix them well together, and pour over the whole the Mayonnaise dressing, beating it through the apple and celery, so that the dressing adheres well to the pieces of the two ingredients.

Miss DOUGLAS, 133 Queen's Gate, London.

WORLD SALAD.

2 fair-sized potatoes boiled and sliced, 2 hard-boiled eggs sliced, 1 Portugal onion very well boiled and pulled in pieces, three anchovies cut in small pieces, 6 large olives, 3 blades of celery boiled till soft and cut in good-sized pieces,—then all to be covered with a good Mayonnaise sauce made about the consistency of double cream.

Miss CAMPBELL of Jura.

TO COOK YAMS.

Boil 2 hours, roast 2 hours ; cut in two, scoop out the inside, and pass it through a sieve. Mix with pepper, salt, cayenne, and a little cream (or milk and butter) till soft enough, like *very* thick sauce. Put in a pan to heat on the fire, then fill the skins with it. Keep very hot and serve.

BEECHWOOD.

ADDITIONAL RECIPES.

Folklore and Mythology Archive

Savouries
and Breakfast Dishes.

ABERDEEN TOAST.

4 oatcakes	1 oz. butter
Bloater paste	Cayenne
White of 1 and yolks of 2 eggs	

Make the oatcakes quite hot, melt the butter, add the eggs, the bloater paste and cayenne; stir till thick, pile on hot biscuits, sprinkle with browned crumbs, and serve at once.

Miss REED, Horsham.

BREAKFAST DISH.

1 onion	Red pepper
6 tomatoes	A very little allspice
3 potatoes	Lard
A slice of ham	Butter
Some grated cheese	Eggs

Fry the sliced onion lightly in some lard and butter mixed, add the tomatoes and ham, both cut in small pieces. When they are well browned add some water and then the potatoes, having first cut them into dice. Let all cook until the potatoes are done, then just before serving mix in grated cheese well flavoured with red pepper, until the sauce is "ropy." Have a very hot dish, pour the sauce on it. Serve carefully poached eggs on the top.

Mrs. CHARLES BRUCE.

CANAPÉS OF FRESH COD ROE.

1 quarter lb. fresh cod roe	3 or 4 slices of bread
1 tablespoonful of thick cream	Salt, cayenne, and lemon juice
Truffle, lobster coral or parsley	

Wash the roe and lay it in a saucepan with enough cold water to cover it, simmer the roe for 5 to 8 minutes, according to the thickness. Next take it out of the water, dry it, and pound till it is a smooth paste. Add the whipped cream and season carefully; strain the lemon juice before adding it. Stamp out rounds from the bread the size of half-a-crown, and fry these a light brown in butter or dripping. Put a little heap of the fish and cream on each croûton, and heat them till very hot in a sharp oven. Sprinkle the tops with chopped truffle or parsley, or washed, dried, pounded, and sieved lobster coral, which when so treated yields a beautiful scarlet powder; or a mixture of these different garnishes has an excellent effect.

CHEESE AIGRETTES.

½ pint of cold water	3 ozs. of grated cheese
1 oz. of butter	Salt, cayenne
3 ozs. of Coomb's flour	3 eggs

Put the water and butter in a stewpan to boil; when boiling stir in the flour, and beat till perfectly smooth; cook till it leaves the sides of the stewpan; when a little cool add the eggs, beating each one in before adding the next; stir in 2 ozs. of cheese, cayenne, and salt. Drop small portions into fat not quite smoking hot, and turn when they rise to the top; fry a golden brown, and drain on kitchen paper. Serve in a pyramid on a serviette, with the remainder of the cheese sprinkled over. For frying in deep fat, melt 1 or 2 lbs. of Hugons suet in a saucepan, remove at once from the fire after using, and strain when cool. It will last for months, and may be clarified when required.

Miss REED, Horsham.

COLD ANCHOVY SAVOURY.

Brown bread	Cream
Seasoning	Anchovies, parsley

Stamp out some bits of brown bread the size of a five shilling piece, pile on each a little stiffly whipped cream (seasoned with salt, pepper, and if liked anchovy essence), lay two boned anchovies crosswise on the top, and decorate with chopped parsley.

Folklore and Mythology Archive

CHEESE BISCUITS.

4 ozs. grated cheese	1 teaspoonful of flour of mustard
3 ozs. finely grated breadcrumbs	1 saltspoonful of cayenne
2 ozs. butter	1 saltspoonful of white pepper
2 beaten up eggs	

Melt the butter and mix all the ingredients together, and let them stand an hour. Knead and work out the paste as thin as possible, and cut into triangles, or roll it up into thin sticks about 3 inches long. Bake in a quick oven from 16 to 18 minutes. Serve hot.

Mrs. BRODRICK, Liverpool.

CHEESE CUSTARD. 1.

5 ozs. of Dunlop cheese	½ a gill of cream or good milk
1 egg, well beaten	

Put the cheese and cream into a pan and stir on the fire till it is melted. Take off the fire and let it stand for a few minutes, then mix in the egg. Mix all well together and pour into a shallow fire-proof dish, and bake in a brisk oven for about 10 minutes. Pieces of nice crisp toast should be handed with the custard.

Miss CAMPBELL of Jura.

CHEESE CUSTARD. 2.

¼ lb. good cheese	Yolks of 2 eggs
Butter, the size of a walnut	Nearly a cupful of milk
Cayenne	

Grate the cheese, put in a saucepan with the butter. Make custard of the eggs and milk. Add the cheese and a little cayenne. Stir it over the fire till it boils. Put in a small pie dish, and brown before the fire.

Mrs. W. E. CRUM.

CHEESE FRITTERS.

About 1 pint water	Flour
Butter, the size of an egg	¼ lb. Parmesan cheese (ground)
A dust of cayenne	Yolks of 3 or 4 and white of 2 eggs
Plenty of black pepper	Hot fat, fine salt

Put water, butter, cayenne, and pepper into saucepan ; when it boils through sift gradually into it sufficient flour to form a thick paste ; take it off the fire, and work into it the cheese, then the yolks, and the whites beaten up to a froth. Then let the paste rest for a couple of hours. Proceed to fry by dropping pieces of it the size of a walnut into plenty of hot fat. Serve sprinkled with fine salt. Mrs. BRODRICK, Liverpool.

CHEESE PANCAKES

4 oz. flour
2 eggs
½ pint milk
2 tablespoonfuls grated Parmesan cheese

2 tablespoonfuls grated Gruyère cheese
1 large tablespoonful cream
Salt
Cayenne and nutmeg

Put the flour, with a dust of salt, in a basin, drop the two eggs in the centre of it, and gradually stir in half the milk. Next beat the batter till it bubbles, then add the rest of the milk, and put aside for half-an-hour. Mix the two kinds of cheese, and stir half of the mixture into the batter. Heat the cream, and add to it the remaining cheese, with a little seasoning, ånd stand the pan containing this on the side of the stove so as to get hot. Fry the batter in a little butter or lard, exactly as you would ordinary pancakes (only keep them quite small, about 3 inches long), and when a nice brown colour on both sides, turn them on to a piece of paper on which has been sprinkled a little grated cheese, and spread over each a thin layer of the cheese and cream mixture. Roll them up neatly, and serve immediately. Miss HUGHES.

CHEESE PUDDING.

6 oz. grated cheese
2 eggs

1 oz. butter
A small teacupful of milk

Beat up all together in a basin. Put into a small baking dish, and bake a light brown. Mrs. BRODRICK.

CHEESE PUDDING.

1 breakfast-cupful of bread-crumbs
3 oz. of grated cheese

Seasoning

2 oz. of butter
½ pint of milk
2 eggs

Boil milk, pour it over the cheese and breadcrumbs, stir in the butter and add the eggs when cool. Bake 20 to 30 minutes. Miss REED, Horsham.

CHEESE EGGS.

2 eggs	1 tablespoonful cream or white sauce
About 1 oz. cheese	Seasoning
Parsley	

Boil the eggs hard, mix the yolks with the other ingredients, replace in the halved whites, bake 10 minutes to quarter of an hour, sprinkle chopped parsley round rims.

Miss YEATMAN.

CHEESE SOUFFLÉS.

½ oz. fresh butter	About 3 oz. grated Parmesan
1 tablespoonful flour	cheese
Milk	Yolks of 3 and whites of 5
White pepper, salt	eggs

Melt butter in saucepan, stir in flour, and when the two are well amalgamated put in a small quantity of milk and the cheese, Stir on a slow fire till it assumes the appearance of thick cream, but be careful not to let it boil. Add pepper, mix thoroughly, add salt if required. Keep on stirring at a very moderate heat for about 10 minutes. Take off the fire, and stir occasionally till quite cold; then stir in the yolks beaten with a little milk and strained, add the whites beaten to a froth. Half-fill some paper cases with the mixture, put them into the oven. and bake for 10 to 15 minutes.

Mrs. BRODRICK.

COLD CHEESE SOUFFLÉS.

1 gill double cream	1½ oz. grated cheese
½ gill aspic jelly	Salt and pepper to taste
A little coloured aspic jelly (carmine) to decorate	

Beat cream very slightly, then add aspic jelly, melted but cold, and the grated cheese, a little pepper, salt and cayenne. Then pour into little soufflé cases. Wet a piece of white paper, and on it chop up the coloured jelly very finely; remove to a plate and, when mixture in cases is quite firm, put a little border of coloured jelly round each. Put a sprig of cress or parsley in centre of each.

Mrs. STEWART, Creich, Fairlie.

CHEESE STRAWS.

2 oz. butter	Yolk of 1 egg
2 oz. flour	A little milk or water
2½ oz. of grated cheese	Seasoning

Rub butter into flour, add the other ingredients (milk last), roll out thin, cut and bake in a slow oven.

Miss HUGHES.

CHICKEN LIVERS.

Chop up the raw livers with a little bacon fat and fry, then serve on buttered toast, with pepper and salt.

Mrs. CHAS. BRUCE.

DEVILS ON HORSEBACK.

Cook some prunes and when cold stone them. Roll each prune in a piece of bacon about five inches long. Tie a bit of thread round each, bake a nice brown, or you can fry them. When ready, take away thread and stick a silver skewer into each.

Mrs. STEWART, Creich, Fairlie.

DEVILLED BONES.

Cut the remains of a fowl or other bones into neat pieces, scoring any flesh on them right through to the bone, then dip them in hot oil or liquefied butter, dust them thickly with mustard flour and " devil pepper," and broil over a sharp, clear fire, basting them from time to time with a little oil or liquefied butter. Curry powder may be used instead of mustard flour.

Devil pepper is made of 1 teaspoonful each of cayenne, salt, and freshly-ground black pepper.

Mrs. W. E. CRUM

DEVILLED BISCUITS.

Butter captain or water biscuits on both sides, and sprinkle well with salt and pepper. Make a slice of cheese into paste with a little made mustard, and cover one side of the biscuit with this. Dust with cayenne, broil, and serve very hot. Pounded anchovy or chutney may be used instead of cheese.

Miss GRAHAM, Sen.,
20 Allan Park, Stirling,

WHITE DEVIL.

1 gill cream whipped stiff	1 dessert-spoonful Worcester
1 dessert-spoonful made	sauce
mustard	1 dessert-spoonful Harvey
Cayenne pepper and salt	sauce

Warm your game as you would for devilling, then put it on the dish you are to send to table. Pour this mixture over, and bake for about five minutes in a quick oven.

Miss PENNIFOLD,
32 Old Queen Street, Westminster.

EGG BUTTER.

Pound together the hard-boiled yolks of 3 eggs, 3 oz. butter, 4 filleted anchovies, a dust of coraline pepper, and a saltspoonful French mustard. Rub it all through a wire sieve and use.

Mrs. BRODRICK.

Eggs à la Provengale.

Put some oil or fat into a frying pan, and when very hot break an egg into a cup, season it with pepper and slide it very gently into the oil. When the egg is a good brown on one side, turn it, and when the other side has browned equally, remove and drain it on a sieve. Repeat with as many eggs as are necessary. Serve in an entrée dish. Build the eggs entrée fashion, laying a croûton between each. Pour into the centre a good, thick brown sauce, flavoured with lemon and cayenne.

Mrs. EDWARD PARKER,
14 Atney Road, Putney, S.W.

EGG TRIFLES.

Boil 4 eggs hard; when cold pass through wire sieve. Add rather more than ¼ pint stiffly-whipped cream, and pepper and salt to taste. Fill small cases with the mixture. Mrs. W. E. CRUM.

FANCY EGGS.

| Eggs | | Ham or chicken |
| Chopped tongue | | Finely chopped parsley |

Butter some tiny tin moulds, sprinkle them round with the chopped parsley, etc.; break a fresh egg into each mould and put a little piece of butter on each. Stand the moulds in a stew or frying pan, letting the hot water come nearly to the top of the moulds, and cook in the oven till the eggs are lightly set. Pass a knife round the moulds, and turn them out on a dish on little rounds of toast or fried bread. Pour tomato butter round them, and serve.

Mrs. BEVAN, 18 Sloane Court, London.

EGG RISSOLES.

6 hard-boiled eggs		1 tablespoonful finely minced parsley
Pepper		Some thick white sauce
Salt		Egg and breadcrumbs
	Boiling fat	

Pass the yolks through a wire sieve, mince the whites very fine, then mix together, season, add the parsley, mix well with the sauce, leave till cold, then roll into balls. Egg and breadcrumb them, and fry in boiling fat. Be sure to egg them well over, as they are apt to burst when frying. Miss GRAHAM, Sen., Stirling.

EGGS À LA TRIPE.

Hard-boil two or three eggs. Make a rich white sauce, and flavour it well with grated cheese. Cut eggs into slices and place in a dish, pour over them the sauce, cover with breadcrumbs and a little sprinkle of cheese. Bake in oven till nicely browned.

Mrs. STEWART, Creich, Fairlie.

FAIRY BUTTER.

½ lb. fresh butter	Cayenne
Bunch of parsley	8 sardines
Salt	4 anchovies

Divide the butter into three pieces; first take one piece and work it smoothly with a palette knife, season with salt and cayenne (pinch), then lay it on a plate, a nice square shape. Take the sardines and anchovies, pound them together with the second piece of butter in a mortar, season with pinch of cayenne, then pass through a very fine hair sieve, and lay on the top of the plain butter. For the green butter take a bunch of parsley, washed well, and boil 3 to 5 minutes, pass through hair sieve, and mix with remainder of butter, season to taste, and lay on the anchovy butter. Serve with dry toast as a savoury.

Miss HORNBY, Beechwood, Grassendale.

Frittata alla Maddelena (Bread Omelet).

½ teacupful breadcrumbs	6 eggs
1 teacupful cream	2 or 3 little bits of butter
	A little powdered nutmeg

Put the breadcrumbs, cream, and nutmeg in a stewpan, as soon as the crumbs have absorbed the cream add the eggs, beat all together, adding 2 or 3 little bits of butter, and fry in butter like an ordinary omelet. Serve with sugar powdered over it, or with apricot jam.

Miss STORY, The University, Glasgow.

GOLDEN BUCK.

| ½ lb. good cheese | 2 tablespoonfuls of pepper |
| ½ oz. butter | 1 egg for each person |

Put all except eggs together in a stewpan, stir over the fire till the cheese is dissolved, pour it over small pieces of toasted bread. Put the eggs, *very* lightly poached, on the top, and serve very hot.

Or cheese may be poured *over* eggs.

DERRY ORMOND.

GREEK TOMATO CHEESE.

Melt ½ lb. of cheddar cheese in a pan with an ounce of butter, when quite thin add two tablespoonfuls of tomato

sauce, cayenne, and salt to taste, and serve on squares of
buttered toast very hot.   Miss CAMPBELL of Jura.

IRISH CUSTARD.

Butter a breakfast cup, sprinkle with chopped parsley,
add a little minced fish, seasoned, pour over a custard
made with 1 egg and ¼ pint milk, and steam.

Miss REED, Horsham.

KIDNEY OMELETTE.

Make a nice light savoury omelette, and cook in the usual
way. Have the kidney sliced very fine, and sautéd in
butter and seasoning, and a teaspoonful of cherry wine,
very hot. Place this on the omelette before folding it,
turn it on to dish with some extra good gravy, and serve
hot.   Miss WALDER, Horsham.

MACARONI À LA CRÈME.

¼ lb. macaroni	2 oz. grated Gruyère cheese
2 oz. fresh butter	½ pint cream
2 oz. of grated Parmesan cheese	Pepper, salt

Boil the macaroni, and after draining it put it into a
stewpan with the other ingredients, hold the stewpan
over the fire, gently moving until well mixed and quite
hot. Then shake it up for a short time to make the cheese
fibrous. When a little of it is taken up it ought to part
in small strings hanging from the spoon. Turn it into
a dish and serve at once, without baking.

Mrs. BRODRICK.

MOCK PÂTÉ DE FOIE GRAS.

A piece of garlic	½ lb. calf's liver
Some fat bacon	¼ lb. cold cooked veal
3 shallots	Salt, white pepper

First rub the frying-pan over with a clove of garlic, melt
a good quantity of bacon fat in it, and fry the shallots
finely chopped and the calf's liver cut in dice. When
done, pound all, including the bacon fat, in a mortar, with
the finely chopped veal, season and, when all is fine, press
into jars and cover with melted butter.

Miss STIRLING, Gargunnock, Stirling.

LUXETTE.

(Very good for savouries, or as potted meat; keeps
a long time.)

2 oz. ham	2 oz. bloater
2 oz. tongue	A few anchovies
2 oz. Findon haddock	A lump of butter the size of
2 oz. kippered herring	an egg

Anchovy sauce

Free all from bones and pound in the mortar, then put
through a hair sieve and mix into a fine paste with
anchovy sauce. (Red herring and hard roes can also be
added.) Put into small jars and pour melted butter over.

Mrs. LE CHALLAS, Glenfinart.

ŒUFS À LA VICE.

8 eggs	2 or 3 spoonfuls milk
A little ham or sardine	1 spoonful flour
1 oz. butter	Salt and pepper

Boil the eggs hard, shell them and cut them in half, take
out the yolks and chop them up, mixed with ham or sardine. Make a fairly thick white sauce with the butter,
milk and flour over the fire; take off and mix with the
yolks; fill the white halves, roll in egg (yolk and white
beaten to a froth), breadcrumb and fry in boiling fat.

Miss S. PILKINGTON, Sandside, Caithness.

RAMAKINS.

½ oz. best flour	3 whites and 2 yolks of eggs
½ oz. Parmesan	½ pint cream
½ oz. good butter	½ pint milk

Stir all but the whites over the fire till it forms a paste,
remove and season to taste. Mix the stiffly beaten whites
lightly in, and bake 10 minutes in a quick oven. This
quantity fills 10 cases.

Mrs. PITT-TAYLOR.

SAVOURY OLIVE AND CHEESE.

Olives	2 tablespoonfuls cream
3 eggs	1 tablespoonful grated
1 gill milk	Parmesan

Seasoning

Beat up the eggs, add the milk, cream, and cheese, and
season it. Pour this custard into small buttered moulds

and steam quickly till set, and let them get cold. Make a hollow in the centre of each, slip an olive into it, and cover the opening with a little wad of the custard which has been scooped out. Turn out the moulds. Arrange in a circle and garnish with small salad.

BASHLEY.

FRENCH OMELET (for 4 people).

6 eggs	Sugar and pepper
½ teacupful milk	Piece of butter the size of a chestnut
A little salt	Some minced parsley

Beat up the eggs in a bowl for five minutes, add the milk, salt, sugar and pepper. Melt the butter in a frying-pan, pour in the mixture, and keep stirring *gently* and lightly with a fork, taking care none sticks to the bottom of the pan, until the whole begins to solidify, then leave alone over the fire for a minute before serving. It should require from 3 to 5 minutes according to the fire, and should be slightly browned on one side and almost liquid on the other. Experience is needed as to the exact amount and kind of stirring over the fire required.

Mrs. BURNLEY-CAMPBELL of Ormidale.

PORRIDGE.

1 pint water	Salt to taste
3 tablespoonfuls coarse oatmeal	

Boil the water first. Sprinkle in the meal, stirring all the time. Boil for 3 or 4 minutes, and simmer for an hour or more, stirring occasionally.

SARDINES À L'ITALIENNE.

Yolks of 2 eggs	½ teaspoonful of chutney
¼ lb. of fresh butter	A little salt and cayenne
Sardines	

Put the yolks of eggs into a stewpan with the butter, chutney, salt and cayenne. Stir these over a slow fire till they form a fairly firm paste. Carefully trim each sardine and dry in a cloth, cover them with the above mixture, egg and breadcrumb them, and fry a delicate colour. Dish them on strips of dried toast, and serve *very hot.* Miss CAMPBELL of Jura.

SARDINE SAVOURY.

4 sardines	1 pinch salt
1 pat of butter	1 pinch cayenne
1 hard-boiled egg	A few drops lemon juice

A little grated cheese

Chop 4 sardines, free from skin, oil and bone, pound them with the pat of butter, yolk of egg, pinch of salt and cayenne, and a few drops of lemon juice. Fry 4 rounds of bread, cut about the size of a five-shilling piece. When brown drain thoroughly, heap the sardine mixture on them, decorate with the chopped white of egg, sprinkle with grated cheese, and bake for five minutes in a moderate oven.

Miss HUGHES.

SCOTCH WOODCOCK.

Yolks of 3 eggs	Seasoning
½ gill cream	Anchovy paste

Prepare some hot buttered toast, spread with anchovy paste. Mix the other ingredients, and beat up over fire till thick enough (about 5 minutes), then pour over toast.

Miss HUGHES.

ANOTHER RECIPE.—Melt a small piece of butter in a stewpan and add a spoonful of rich gravy, pepper and salt, and break in two eggs, stirring quickly. When the eggs thicken add a flavouring of anchovy, then pour the mixture on hot toast, and serve.

HORS D'ŒUVRE OF SHRIMPS.

4 tomatoes	Salt and pepper to
1 teaspoonful vinegar	taste
1 claret-glassful light white wine	½ pint shelled shrimps
	Suspicion of onion

Pass tomatoes through sieve and mix well with the wine, vinegar, salt and pepper. Put the shrimps either into an old china bowl or separate little china pattie pans, one for each person, having first rubbed them lightly with an onion. Pour the mixture over the shrimps, set on ice or put in a cold place, and serve cold.

M. P.-S.

TOMATES AUX CHAMPIGNONS.

Butter
1 small shallot
1 teaspoonful of parsley
6 small mushrooms
Pepper
Salt

2 tablespoonfuls brown bread-
   crumbs
3 medium-sized tomatoes
Watercress
(Salad oil, chilli
   Tarragon vinegar)

Fry the chopped shallot and mushrooms in 1 oz. of butter, then add the parsley, pepper, salt, and bread-crumbs. Cut the tomatoes in halves and remove the seeds, fill the hollows with the prepared mixture, put a small piece of butter on each, sprinkle with brown bread-crumbs, and bake in a moderate oven 10 minutes. Serve with watercress, which may be slightly sprinkled with salad oil, chilli, and Tarragon vinegar.

Mrs. BRODRICK.

ADDITIONAL RECIPES.

THE PERFECT WHEAT FOODS.

DAINTY, NOURISHING.

FAROLA is immeasurably superior to arrowroot, corn flour, sago, etc. With milk it forms exquisite puddings, and in the nursery it will prove a valuable variety, which children will take with avidity."

Liverpool Medico-Chirurgical Journal.

" An ideal form of giving farinaceous food with milk."

A London Physician.

AWARDED Gold Medals at the two important International Exhibitions held in 1886—Edinburgh and Liverpool.

FAROLA is a highly refined preparation of Wheat, which conserves all the nutritive elements and fine flavour naturally belonging to the purest part of the grain. All irritating and indigestible matter has been removed by careful treatment, mechanical means only being employed.

FAROLA will satisfy a robust appetite, but it is specially suited for invalids and children.

Is similar in constitution and purity to Farola, but is in the form of large granules, and is therefore specially suited for making such dishes as Porridge, Steamed Pudding, etc.

A gratis and post free Sample will be sent on receipt of Post Card.

JAMES MARSHALL (Glasgow), Ld.,

25 East Cumberland Street, GLASGOW.

PUDDINGS.

ALMOND PASTRY.

4 oz. castor sugar
1 small dessert-spoonful
cornflour

6 oz. almonds
1 teaspoonful of essence of
vanilla

Whites of 2 eggs

Blanch and chop the almonds fine, mix with sugar, beat the whites of the two eggs (not too stiffly), add them to the other ingredients, and lastly add the cornflour and vanilla. Spread thinly on a well-greased baking sheet, and cook in a moderately hot oven for 15 or 20 minutes. When cooked cut in rounds or oval shapes.

Miss HUGHES.

ALMOND PUDDING.

¼ lb. butter
8 eggs
Sugar to taste
2 cupfuls milk

4 cupfuls flour
Rind and juice of half a lemon
⅛ teaspoonful Madeira
½ teaspoonful cream of tartar

Pound the butter, stir in the yolks of eggs and sugar, add slowly the milk and flour, and mix for a short half-hour; then add the almonds, lemon, Madeira, cream of tartar, and lastly add slowly the whites of eggs (beaten). Bake from three-quarters of an hour to an hour.

Frau BRESCA,
Leubnitzer Strasse 16, Dresden.

AMBER PUDDING. 1.

3 eggs
Their weight in butter, sugar,
and flour

Juice of 1 or 2 and grated
peel of 1 lemon

Work the butter with your hand till like cream, then add the flour, sugar, and beaten eggs by degrees, then the lemon juice and peel. Butter a mould quickly, and when the ingredients are well mixed pour them in, taking care that the mould is quite full. Butter a piece of white paper and lay it on the top, tie it well over with a cloth, and put it into a saucepan of fast boiling water. Boil 3 hours.   Miss REED, Horsham.

AMBER PUDDING. 2.

¼ lb. suet.
¼ lb. sugar.
¼ lb. breadcrumbs.
2 tablespoonfuls marmalade.

3 eggs.
3 oz. citron and lemon peel (chopped up)

Beat the whites stiff and add to the other ingredients. Boil 4 hours in a mould and serve with milled sauce.

Milled Sauce.

2 eggs
Wineglassful of sherry
Sugar to taste

Whisk all together in the pan on the fire; never let it boil.

BEECHWOOD.

ANGEL PUDDING.

2 oz. of powdered sugar
2 oz. of fine dried flour
Yolks of 2 and white of 1 egg

Grated rind of half a lemon
½ pint of cream
2 oz. of butter

Melt the butter and the sugar slowly in the cream over the fire, and, when the mixture is nearly cold, pour it gradually over the flour, stirring it all the time to prevent lumps forming. When well mixed add the lemon rind and the beaten yolks of eggs, and lastly, just before baking, the beaten white. Pour the mixture into 12 small moulds, only half filling them. Bake 20 minutes, turn out, and serve immediately.

Miss REED, Horsham.

APPLE CHARLOTTE.

4 or 5 apples
1 lemon
2 oz. butter

Castor sugar to taste
1 oz. of stale bread-crumbs

Well butter a plain mould and sprinkle with brown sugar. Then line the mould with slices of thin bread and butter, then a layer of apples, pared, cored, and cut into thin slices. Sprinkle over these some breadcrumbs and a portion of the grated lemon peel, and juice and sugar, proceeding in this manner until the dish is full. Then pour over 1 oz. of clarified butter, and cover it up with the apple peel to prevent it from burning. Bake in a moderate oven for 1 hour or more. When cooked turn the charlotte carefully on a dish and serve hot.

Miss HUGHES.

CLEAR APPLE.

| 1 quart of apples | 1 lb. sugar |
| 1 pint water | 1 lemon |

Peel and core the apples and cut them into quarters. Put the sugar into a preserving pan with a little water to prevent it from burning, and boil ¼ of an hour ; take off the scum and lay the quarters of apple carefully in the syrup, with some lemon juice. The apples must be good and hard. Bring to the boil once, and then let it stand and simmer for 1½ hours. Remove the quarters of apple and place in a glass dish. Strain the syrup and pour it over the apples. Let it stand till cold and serve. The apples may also be done whole (of course peeling and coring them first) with bits of lemon peel. The great secret is to cook them *slowly*, so that they do not fall to pieces. A certain small, hard, green apple is the best for the purpose, becoming quite transparent. Whipped cream, with red jelly or chopped pistachio nut, may be used to decorate them.

APPLE FOOL.

Bake some good apples, remove the pulp with a spoon, and beat it up with a little sifted sugar. To a teacupful use the yolk of 1 egg and a small spongecake. Mix all together and rub through a sieve.

Mrs. W. E. CRUM.

APPLE JELLY.

24 apples (any kind which is slightly acid)
3 quarts water

Sugar to taste
A little lemon peel if liked
A small packet gelatine

Peel and core the apples, place in a stewpan with the water and lemon, and boil down till reduced to 2 quarts; sweeten. Put the gelatine in cold spring water for 10 minutes, then add to the jelly and boil 10 minutes; strain through a jelly-bag, leave till nearly cold, then put into moulds.

When apples are scarce, the peel and core will do as well as the apples if nicely washed.

BEECHWOOD.

APPLE SHAPE.

2 to 2½ lbs. apples
½ lb. lump sugar

Juice of one lemon

½ oz. gelatine
¼ gill water

Peel and core the apples, put them into an enamelled saucepan, with sugar and water, for 10 minutes; then, when quite cooked, put the apple pulp through a hair sieve into a basin; then add gelatine and lemon juice (the gelatine must be melted in a little water before adding). Put into a china or copper mould. The mould must first be well damped with cold water. May be served with custard or whipped cream.

Miss HUGHES.

APPLE SOUFFLÉ.

1 gill of apple purée
1 oz. of butter

½ oz. of flour
Yolks of 2, whites of 3 eggs

1 tablespoonful of thick cream

To make purée, cook four apples in a little water, sweeten to taste, and when soft rub through a hair sieve. Melt the butter in a saucepan, stir in the flour, and then add the purée. Cook well, stirring all the time. Take off the fire, and when slightly cool add 2 yolks of eggs and the cream; beat these in very thoroughly, then whip the whites of 3 eggs to a stiff froth, and stir in very lightly. Turn the mixture into a well-greased soufflé tin, with oiled paper round, and steam very gently for half-an-hour.

Folklore and Mythology Archive

Sauce.—½ gill of whipped cream, 1 small teaspoonful of vanilla, a little castor sugar. The whipped cream to be put round the dish when the soufflé is turned out.

Miss Hughes.

ARAB PUDDING.

½ lb. dates		½ pint milk
2 eggs		Sponge cakes
	Almonds	

Cook dates till soft, put an almond in place of each stone. Make a custard of the eggs and milk, and beat in the sponge cake. Cook for about 10 minutes, mix in the dates, and serve hot, with whipped cream flavoured with lemon put on the top as it comes to table. The pudding to be hot, the cream to be cold.

S. C.

BAKED CUSTARD.

Into a pint-and-a-half of milk stir three tablespoonfuls of Farola, two ounces of butter, and three-and-a-half ounces of sugar, with the grated rind of a lemon. Boil for five minutes, stirring all the time. Beat the yolks and whites of four eggs separately; stir them into the mixture while it is still hot. Bake for half-an-hour in a moderate oven.

James Marshall, Ltd.

BAKED PUDDING.

Mix carefully half a pound of Cerola in half a pint of cold milk. Heat two pints of milk short of boiling; add the Cerola and milk. Mix in 3 ounces of butter, 3 ounces of sugar, a little grated lemon rind, and four eggs previously beaten. Bake for half-an-hour in a moderate oven.

James Marshall, Ltd.

BAKEWELL PUDDING.

10 eggs
½ lb. of sugar
½ lb. of butter

A little jam
Essence of almonds
Puff paste

Having covered the dish with thin puff paste, put on it a layer of jam half-an-inch thick. Take the yolks of 8 eggs, the whites of 2, the melted butter, sugar, and essence of almonds to taste, beat all well together, pour the mixture into the dish one inch thick, and bake one hour in a moderate oven.

Miss REED, Horsham.

BAKEWELL TARTS.

Take some tin plates, about eight inches in diameter, butter them, and line with the following sweet paste, or with puff paste.

SWEET PASTE.—1 lb. flour, 8 oz. butter, 8 oz. castor sugar, 1 egg. Make into paste with as little handling as possible, as that makes the paste tough. Now on the paste spread a spoonful of jam (greengage is the best), then place in a bowl 8 oz. butter and 8 oz. castor sugar, and beat up well, adding 6 eggs, 2 at a time. When ready add the flours, 6 oz. patent and 6 oz. plain well mixed, well mix together, and cover the jam nicely and levelly. Bake in a cool oven, it will take one hour. When cold some can be iced with water icing, flavoured with vanilla, and some can have blanched almonds on top, and some can have desiccated cocoanut, coloured green, sprinkled on the white icing before it quite sets hard.

Mr. THOMAS HILL,
12 Gladstone Road, Seacombe.

BABA À LA ST. JACQUES.

1 lb. flour
½ oz. German yeast
½ lb. butter
8 eggs

½ lb. powdered sugar
1 oz. chopped citron
1 oz. currants
Pinch of salt

2 oz. sultanas

Take a quarter of a pound of flour, make a well in the centre, stir in ½ oz. of German yeast dissolved in water, roll it into a ball, and keep it in a warm place wrapped

in a cloth till it has risen to twice its usual size. Take
$\frac{3}{4}$ lb. of flour, $\frac{1}{2}$ lb. of butter, 3 eggs, $\frac{1}{2}$ lb. of powdered
sugar and a pinch of salt, stir well together, add 5 eggs,
one after the other, then the ball of yeast, the chopped
citron, currants and sultanas. Knead the paste thoroughly
and put it into a mould capable of holding twice the
quantity, leave it until it has risen to nearly the top of
the mould, bake, and when done turn out of the mould
and cover with the following sauce:—Dissolve some
apricot jam in a tumblerful of clarified sugar and a large
wineglassful of sherry (or rum), and boil till it is a thick
sauce.

Mrs. EDWARD PARKER,
14 Atney Road, Putney, S.W.

BARONESS PUDDING.

$\frac{3}{4}$ lb. suet	$\frac{3}{4}$ lb. flour
$\frac{3}{4}$ lb. raisins, weighed after being stoned	$\frac{3}{4}$ pint of milk
	$\frac{1}{4}$ saltspoonful of salt

Chop the suet fine, stone the raisins, cut them into halves,
mix with the salt and flour, and moisten with milk.
Stir the mixture well, then tie the pudding in a floured
cloth previously wrung out in boiling water, put the
pudding into a saucepan of boiling water, and let it boil
$4\frac{1}{2}$ hours. Serve with plain sifted sugar.

Miss REED, Horsham.

FRENCH BATTER PUDDING.

2 oz. butter	2 oz. sugar
2 oz. flour	$\frac{1}{2}$ pint milk, 2 eggs

Work the butter to a cream, add the rest, the milk last of
all, flavour to taste. Bake half-an-hour.

BEECHWOOD.

CARROT PUDDING.

1 large carrot	1 large spoonful orange flower
A spoonful of biscuit powder	or rosewater
Yolks of 4 and whites of 2 eggs	2 oz. sugar
1 pint cream	A little ratafia

Boil the carrot till soft, bruise it in a marble mortar, mix
with other ingredients. Bake in a shallow dish. Turn
it out, and serve with sugar over it.

BEECHWOOD.

BAKED OR BOILED CARROT PUDDING.

½ lb. breadcrumbs	¼ lb. currants
4 oz. suet	3 oz. sugar
¼ lb. raisins (stoned)	3 eggs
¾ lb. carrots	Milk and nutmeg

Boil carrots until tender enough to mash to a pulp, add the remaining ingredients, and moisten with sufficient milk to make the pudding of the consistency of thick batter. If to be boiled put the mixture into a buttered basin, tie it down with a cloth, and boil 2½ hours. If to be baked put it into a pie dish, and bake for nearly an hour. Turn out on a dish and strew sifted sugar over it.

Miss REED, Horsham.

BANANAS.

The following recipes are published by kind permission of The West Indian Produce Association, 4 Fenchurch Buildings, E.C., and are copyright :—

BANANAS.—Cut about a quarter of an inch from each end, but do not peel the bananas. Lay them in a baking dish and bake them in a hot oven for about 15 minutes. When done the skin should burst open like that of a baked apple. Then turn the bananas over and bake for 5 minutes on the other side. Serve very hot. *Another method* is to remove a strip of the skin, cutting off each end as before, and place in a shallow pan with the exposed side up. Mix two tablespoonfuls of Wipa cane sugar, two of melted butter, and two of lime juice with a pinch of salt, and baste the bananas with this, while they are baking, for 15 to 20 minutes till soft. Heat the remainder of the dressing and pour over the bananas. Serve very hot.

BANANAS (Dried).—Wipa dried bananas are very sustaining, and are becoming increasingly popular. They are largely used in America, especially for invalids. They may be eaten as they are for dessert, or cooked or steamed as follows :—

BANANAS à la Trinidad.—Stew the bananas, place them in a pie dish and let them steep in 3 glasses of sherry, 2 oz. white sugar, half a nutmeg (grated), the thin rind of a lime, and a teaspoonful of pounded cloves. Roll each banana in sifted flour. Fry in boiling lard. Drain and serve with sugar.

BANANA BOILED PUDDINGS.—8 oz. of dried bananas cut in small slices, 6 oz. of breadcrumbs, 4 oz. sugar, 4 oz. of suet chopped fine, 2 eggs, ½ pint milk. Mix and beat up with a wooden spoon for 10 minutes. Boil in a mould for 4 hours, and serve plain or with sweet sauce.

BANANA FRITTERS.—Soak 2 bananas in warm water till soft and then mash. Add 1 egg, 1 teaspoonful of flour, and 4 of milk. Then fry.

BANANA PANCAKES.—Cut sufficient bananas into small pieces. Stew with a little white wine, grated lime peel and sugar to taste. Spread the mixture over the pancakes. Roll up and serve with sifted sugar.

BANANAS STEWED.—Take 2 bananas for each person. Steam until the bananas swell and become soft. Then stew with enough good butter to fry lightly; when brown, add sugar equal in weight to the bananas, and by degrees warm water to make a syrup. Simmer in the thickening syrup until cool.

BANANA BISCUITS.—Mix and knead thin 1½ lbs. of banaflor, ½ lb. of wheat flour, ½ lb. sugar, 2 eggs, 1 spoonful of butter, and 1 of lard. Add essence to taste. Mix, knead thin and bake.

CHARLOTTE RUSSE.

Sponge fingers	½ oz. gelatine
½ pint cream	3 eggs
2 oz. castor sugar	2 tablespoonfuls maraschino
A piece of split vanilla pod	Rather better than ¼ pint milk

Line a plain mould with a well-oiled paper, trim some sponge finger biscuits and place them round the mould close together. Then prepare a custard to fill up the centre. Put rather more than a quarter pint of milk in a pan, just bring it to the boil with the castor sugar and vanilla, then stand it in the bain-marie to infuse. Dissolve in it the gelatine, and stir it on to the raw yolks of eggs. Thicken over the fire, being careful it does not boil; when cool add a quarter pint of thick whipped cream and maraschino. Fill up the mould with the mixture, and, when set, turn it out and serve on a dish garnished with whipped cream, by means of a bag or fancy pipe.

Miss REED, Horsham.

HOT CHESTNUT PUDDING.

1 lb. chestnuts	Yolks of 4 and whites of 3
4 oz. butter	eggs
4 oz. sugar	Whipped cream
½ pint milk	Vanilla flavouring

Boil the chestnuts, remove the skins, and pass through a sieve. Melt the butter in a stewpan and then add the chestnuts, sugar and milk. Stir gently over the fire till it begins to thicken, then stir rapidly till it begins to leave the sides of the pan, then remove from the fire. When a little cool add the yolks and whipped whites of eggs, steam for 2 hours, and serve with whipped cream over it, flavoured with vanilla.

Mrs. BRODRICK.

CHINESE RICE.

2 oz. of rice	½ oz. of gelatine
1½ pints of milk	½ pint of cream
2 oz. of butter	Sugar to taste

Boil rice in a pint of milk until quite soft, add butter and sugar, dissolve gelatine in ¼ pint of milk and add to the rest. When quite cold stir in the cream and put into a mould.

Miss REED, Horsham.

CHOCOLATE CREAM.

1 oz. powdered chocolate	1½ ozs. castor sugar
1 tablespoonful of milk	½ pint double cream
A little desiccated cocoanut	

Dissolve chocolate in the milk by warming, mix this with the cream and sugar, whip the whole until quite stiff, pour into a perforated china mould lined with wetted muslin, allow to stand 12 hours; turn out, remove the muslin and sprinkle with the desiccated cocoanut.

Mrs. BRODRICK.

CHOCOLATE PUDDING.

3 eggs
Their weight in flour, sugar,
and butter (*i.e.*, weight of
1 egg to each ingredient)

1 oz. chocolate
Carbonate of soda to cover
a sixpenny bit.

Beat butter to a cream, add eggs and stir well, add flour, then chocolate, butter a tin and a piece of paper to cover it, pour in the mixture, cover with paper and a damp cloth and tie it down, steam gently for 1½ to 2 hours.

Sauce (to be poured over just before serving)—

1 oz. chocolate | Yolk of 1 egg (whipped) | ½ gill milk

This pudding can wait if left in pan.

Mrs. WATSON.

Marmalade Pudding.

Same ingredients as above, but substitute marmalade for chocolate.

CHOCOLATE GENOESE.

¼ lb. of flour
¼ lb. of butter

¼ lb. of sugar, 5 eggs
¼ lb. chocolate

Mix as for pound cake. Put into a sauté pan, and bake in rather a quick oven.

Miss A. PENNIFOLD,
32 Old Queen Street, Westminster.

COCOANUT PUDDING.

6 ozs. of grated cocoanut
4 ozs. of powdered sugar
2 ozs. of butter

Rind and juice of 1 lemon
½ pint of milk
4 eggs, puff paste

Put the cocoanut, butter and sugar in a saucepan on the fire, when dissolved add the milk and the grated rind of lemon. Boil for one minute. Remove from the fire and add the eggs well beaten, and the lemon juice. Have ready a shallow pie dish, lined with puff paste, pour in the mixture, and bake for an hour.

Miss REED.

COFFEE CAKE SWEET.

A spongecake	About ½ gill milk
Butter	1 pint cream
Sugar	Essence of coffee

Having made a spongecake, cut it into three, spread butter and sugar beaten to a cream on each slice, put them together again and soak in a little milk. Then whip up the cream, divide it and put a little essence of coffee in half of it. Put first coffee cream and then white cream on the cake until it is quite covered.

Miss SANDBACH, Stoneleigh, Rossett.

COFFEE CREAM.

1 teacupful *strong* coffee	2 oz. of sugar
½ oz. of gelatine	1 gill cream

Melt the gelatine and sugar in the coffee, let it cool, strain through muslin (previously wrung out in tepid water), whip the cream (three minutes or so), and add to the coffee. Mix gently round, and when cool pour into mould.

If you pour it too soon into the mould, before it is a certain thickness, the coffee will settle at the bottom.

In making chocolate or other creams melt the gelatine in a little water, and add last.

Miss HUGHES, Beechwood.

COFFEE PUDDING.

¼ lb. of flour	½ pint of coffee
¼ lb. of butter	2 small eggs
2 oz. of sugar	¼ teaspoonful baking powder

Cream the butter, add the sugar, then the eggs, then the baking powder, and lastly the coffee. Beat well together, and steam for one hour. Be very careful not to let it boil.

SAUCE FOR PUDDING.—Make an ordinary custard, and add one teacupful of strong coffee. Pour over the pudding.

Miss YEATMAN.

Folklore and Mythology Archive

Another Recipe.

2 oz. butter		1 egg
2 oz. sugar		1 tablespoonful essence of coffee
4 oz. flour		1 teaspoonful of baking powder
	A little milk	

Cream butter and sugar, add flour and beaten-up egg alternately, then a little milk till a thick batter is formed, then coffee, and lastly baking powder. Mix well. Butter a basin, and steam 1½ hours. Serve with sauce as above.

Mrs. STEWART, Creich, Fairlie.

COFFEE SOUFFLÉ.

About ½ pint of cream or milk		10 oz. of sugar
6 oz. flour		Yolks of 5 and whites of 6 or 7
¼ pint very strong coffee		eggs
	A little salt	

Bring the cream to the boil, add the flour (previously well mixed with milk), and when it thickens add the coffee, sugar and yolks of eggs, and a little salt. When nearly cold add the well-whipped whites of egg, and bake in a good oven, but not too fierce at first.

BEECHWOOD.

CRÊME BRÛLÉE.

1 pint cream		Powdered sugar
	Yolks of 4 very fresh eggs	

Boil the cream for 1 minute, pour on it the yolks of eggs, well beaten, then put it again on the fire and let it just come to the boil. Pour it into the dish in which it is to be served and let it get cold. Strew a thick crust of powdered sugar over it, put it in a slow oven for 10 minutes, then brown it with a salamander and serve it cold. The dish ought to be a *very* shallow one.

Mrs. CHAS. BRUCE.

DEVONSHIRE JUNKET.

About ¼ lb. lump sugar		1 tablespoonful rennet
1 wineglassful sherry or brandy		Nutmeg
1 quart new milk		Scalded or whipped cream

Put the sugar into a glass or china dish, pour on the wine, then add the milk warmed, and rennet. Mix the whole together, grate over a little nutmeg, and when cold add the cream on top.

Mrs. SANDBACH,
85 Cadogan Gardens, London.

Pianofortes & Organs.

PIANO-PLAYERS.

THE Largest Stock of Musical Instruments in the United Kingdom on Sale, Hire, or Deferred Payment System. Instruments returned from Hire at Reduced Prices. Illustrated Catalogue on application.

PATERSON, SONS & Co.,
152 BUCHANAN STREET,
GLASGOW,

Ayr, Dumfries, Paisley, Kilmarnock, Greenock, and Oban.

DUCHESS LOAVES.

½ gill water	1½ oz. castor sugar
2 oz. butter	3 small eggs
3 oz. flour	Almonds Cream

Bring the butter, water, and sugar to the boil, stir in the flour, let it simmer 10 minutes (stirring occasionally). When nearly cold add the eggs (stir each in separately). Put small spoonfuls of this mixture on a greased baking tin; bake in medium oven 20 minutes (they fall if baked too quickly). Egg them, and cover with chopped almonds, and fill between the two halves with whipped cream.

This is the same mixture as for chocolate éclairs.

Miss HUGHES, Beechwood.

ELOISE PUDDING.

8 oz. bread	2 oz. coarse sago
6 oz. suet	3 eggs
5 oz. moist sugar	1 large tablespoonful marmalade
Milk	Raisins

Steep sago in milk 4 or 5 hours, mix with other ingredients. Ornament a mould with raisins, put in the pudding; boil in plenty of water 6 hours.

Serve with currant jelly or wine sauce.

BEECHWOOD.

ESSEX PUDDING.

4 oz. sugar	1 teaspoonful baking powder
3 oz. butter	2 eggs
5 oz. flour	Milk, jam or syrup

Beat butter and sugar to a cream, add flour gradually and the eggs well beaten, then enough milk to make it the consistency of thick cream. Butter a mould, and spread jam round it, pour in the mixture and steam 1½ hours, or omit the jam, and when cooked pour over it hot golden syrup.

Mrs. BEVAN, 18 Sloane Court, London.

CROÛTES AU BARON.

A croûton fried crisp, with a mushroom the same size laid on it, and a piece of soft herring's roe on the top. Serve very hot.

Mrs. ARTHUR H. BRADSHAW,
38 Kensington Gardens Square, London.

AN EXCELLENT CREAM.

⅔ of a pint of very rich cream
Lemon peel
A squeeze of lemon juice

½ a glass of sweet wine
Sugar to taste
Puff paste biscuits

Macaroons

Whip up the cream to a strong froth with some finely scraped lemon peel, the lemon juice, wine, and sugar to make it pleasant, but not too sweet, lay it on a sieve or in a form, and next day put it on a dish and ornament it with very light puff paste biscuits, made in shapes the length of a finger and about two thick, over which sugar may be strewed or a little glaze with isinglass, or you may use macaroons to line the edges of the dish.

Mrs. W. E. Crum.

FIG PUDDING.

2 eggs
Their weight in butter and flour
Shreds of lemon peel

Sugar to taste
½ teaspoonful of baking powder
Some stewed figs

Beat the butter and sugar to a cream, add the eggs, and lastly the flour and baking powder (mixed). Butter a shallow basin, cover the bottom with the stewed figs and pour the batter over. Bake 20 to 30 minutes. As nice cold as hot. Other fruit may be used.

Miss Reed, Horsham.

CREAM OF FIGS.

¼ lb. dried figs
1 small glassful of claret

Sugar to sweeten
½ pint whipped cream

6 sheets gelatine

Stew the figs in the claret and sugar, pass through a hair sieve, then add the cream and gelatine.

Miss A. Pennifold,
32 Old Queen Street, Westminster.

FLAN ANGLAIS AU CARAMEL.

1 pint milk
Yolks of 6 and whites of 3 eggs

A few lumps white sugar
A *little* water

Flavouring to taste

Make an ordinary custard of eggs and milk, flavouring with whatever you like. Have a small enamel-lined pan with a flat cover. Put in the sugar and a very little water, only enough to moisten the sugar, and let it be on the stove till it begins to assume a bright gold tinge, then take it off or it will speedily turn black. Very soon it will be a nice bright brown, and then add as much water as it will bear; it must not taste watery, nor must it be syrup—only practice will guide you as to quantity. You must turn and twist the pan till the caramel covers the sides all round, then pour in the custard, put on the lid, on the top of which you must strew hot embers, let it do gently for half-an-hour or more. It turns out well, and can be eaten hot, but is better cold.

FRENCH RECIPE.

"Spun Glass" to decorate above Pudding.

¼ lb. lump sugar, ½ gill water, juice of half a small lemon.

Let these simmer till melted to a syrup, then boil about a quarter of an hour, till brown. Test by letting drops of it fall into cold water; when these become brittle allow the mixture to cool slightly, then take some on a fork in your right hand, and taking a little of the caramel from the fork between the finger and thumb of your left hand, draw it slowly away. If of the right consistency it will pull out as thin as a hair, a yard long. Coil this on the left hand till it breaks, then start again. If there are lumps break them off. Finally arrange lightly in coils on the pudding, about 6 or 8 inches high. Some cooks whisk up the caramel with a fork over a large sheet of paper, but this is more difficult. It will only stand about five minutes, but the caramel can be made beforehand and re-heated.

FRUIT TRANSPARENCY.

| 1 quart fresh currants | | ½ oz. gelatine |
| ¼ lb. loaf sugar | | 1 pint fresh fruit |

Press out the juice of the currants, strain it through a fine sieve into a brass skillet, add sugar and gelatine, boil and skim till perfectly bright and rather thick, about 20 minutes. Pour into a pretty mould and stir in fresh fruit; put in a cool place or on ice till quite firm. Turn out carefully, and serve with or without Devonshire or other cream round as a garnish. If *red* currant juice be used let the fruit be either red currants, raspberries, or red cherries; if *white* currant juice, either strawberries or white currants.

BEECHWOOD.

GERACLIFFE CREAM.

1 oz. gelatine	Rinds of 2 oranges and 1 lemon
1 quart milk	(peeled very fine)
Sugar to taste	Yolks of 2 eggs

Boil the rinds of oranges and lemon in as little water as possible with the gelatine for half-an-hour, strain, and when quite cool add it to the milk and yolks and sugar. Put it in a saucepan and let it get thoroughly hot, but *not* boil. Put in a mould to set. This is enough for two shapes.

SYRUP.—Grated rinds of 2 oranges and juice of 4, the rind and juice of 1 lemon, $\frac{1}{4}$ lb. loaf sugar. Boil up for a quarter of an hour. When cold pour over the cream.

Mrs. J. TINNE, Bashley Lodge, New Forest.

GINGER APPLES.

6 lbs. apples (hard and juicy)	$\frac{1}{4}$ lb. whole ginger
4 lbs. white sugar	$\frac{1}{2}$ lb. bruised ginger

1 pint water

Prepare and quarter the apples. Fill a jar with alternate layers of apples, sugar, and whole ginger. Cover it over and leave it standing 48 hours to harden. Infuse the bruised ginger in boiling water for 24 hours, then strain through muslin, and put into it the contents of the jar. Boil for three-quarters or one hour.

BEECHWOOD.

GINGER PUDDING.

$\frac{1}{4}$ lb. butter, $\frac{1}{2}$ lb. flour, 2 eggs, 3 tablespoonfuls of treacle, $\frac{1}{2}$ glass of milk, teaspoonful of ginger, $\frac{1}{2}$ teaspoonful of carbonate of soda, $\frac{1}{4}$ teaspoonful of cream of tartar. Steam two hours.

Mrs. BRODRICK.

Folklore and Mythology Archive

GOOSEBERRY FOOL.

1 pint picked gooseberries, 5 oz. castor sugar, ¼ pint cream.

Place the gooseberries and sugar in a jar in the oven (with *no* water) till the fruit is soft, then pass them through a hair sieve into a basin and mix in the cream.

ICED SOUFFLÉ.

1 pint cream	Jam	5 eggs

Beat the cream and whites of eggs (separately) till they are stiff; mix some jam with the yolks, sweeten to taste, and put all together into the soufflé tin, which must be put ready previously as follows: Put a layer of the same jam as already used at the bottom; then oil a paper and line the tin with it, so that it stands 1½ inches above the tin all round. Fill with the mixture to the top of the paper. Then pack in ice and freeze.

BEECHWOOD.

ICED SOUFFLÉ PUDDING.

½ pint new milk	1 tablespoonful brandy
Yolks of 4 eggs	1 pint cream
¼ lb. ratafias	A little grated spongecake

Make a custard with the milk and eggs, then put into it the ratafias and brandy. Freeze the cream, and fill a round soufflé tin with alternate layers of custard and iced cream. Before serving, grate a little spongecake over the top layer (which should be cream).

A sauce of brandy cherries set on fire may be served with this. BEECHWOOD.

INDIAN FRITTERS.

3 tablespoonfuls flour	3 eggs
Boiling milk to make a stiff	Dripping
paste	Jam or cheesecake mixture

Add the milk to the flour, then the eggs (yolks and whites whipped separately), and beat well together. Drop a spoonful at a time into boiling dripping. When done, open at the side and put some jam in.

BEECHWOOD.

ITALIAN PUDDING (for 6 Persons).

¼ lb. of any plain sweet biscuit
6 macaroons
2 oz. candied peel
1 oz. sultanas

1 oz. pistachio nuts
Yolks of 3 and whites of 8 eggs
½ pint cream
A small glassful rum or liqueur

Pound the biscuits and macaroons, chop the peel, sultanas, and nuts fine, and mix with three whole eggs, the whites of the rest, cream, and liqueur. Put the mixture into a mould, buttered and lined with paper, and cook in a bain-marie for about 1 hour. Punch or sweet sauce may be served with this pudding.

Miss REED, Horsham.

LECHE CRÉMA.

Yolks of 3 and white of 1 egg
1½ pints milk
4 tablespoonfuls fine wheat flour

Cinnamon

2 oz. finely powdered loaf sugar
Grated lemon peel to flavour
½ lb. ratafia cakes

Beat up the eggs and add to them gradually the milk. Then mix carefully the flour, add the sugar and lemon peel. Boil these ingredients over a slow fire, stirring constantly to prevent their burning, until the flour is quite dissolved. Prepare a glass dish with the ratafia cakes at the bottom ; and, when the cream is sufficiently boiled, pour it through a sieve upon the cakes. When quite cold, just before serving, dust some finely-powdered cinnamon over it.

Mrs. W. E. CRUM.

LEMON CHEESECAKE MIXTURE.

4 oz. butter
Rind of 2 and juice of 1½ lemons

½ lb. sugar
Yolks of 3 (and, if liked, whites of 2) eggs

Mix all except eggs, and melt on fire. Add the eggs, well whipped, and stir gently over fire 15 minutes or so (it must not boil). Leave it to thicken. It will keep 3 months.

Miss HUGHES.

LEMON CREAM (delicious).

¾ pint boiling water
¾ lb. lump sugar

¼ pint good cream

Rind and juice of 3 lemons
3 eggs

Pour the boiling water over the lemon rind and juice and sugar (pare your lemons very thin and take off all the white before squeezing out the juice), then mix with it the yolks and whites of eggs. Do this very gradually, or it will turn. Then put the whole into an earthenware saucepan and let it simmer very gently over a slow fire, stirring all the time, till it becomes as thick as custard. Strain into a jug and when cold add the cream.

Mrs. GEORGE BROWN, Châlet Fairlie, Pau.

BOILED LEMON CREAM.

1 pint of cream		Sugar to taste
Rind of 2 lemons		Large teaspoonful of flour
	Yolks of 4 eggs	

Boil the cream, lemon rind, sugar, and flour; when boiling, have the yolk of eggs whipped in a basin, pour the above into it, stirring all the time; put it out to cool. When cold, butter a plain mould, not too thickly, put the cream into it and steam it for an hour and let it go cold.

Mrs. W. E. CRUM.

LEMON CURD.

Rinds of 2 and juice of 6		1½ pints water
lemons		2½ lbs. lump sugar
4 oz. fresh butter		9 eggs
2 oz. arrowroot		A few drops acetic acid

Put the water in kettle, add sugar, butter, and inside of the lemons, and the rinds of two of the lemons. Boil, take off the fire and gradually add the eggs. When well beaten up bring to the boil again, then add the arrowroot, stirring well, and boil for 5 minutes more; add a few drops of acetic acid (or a very small pinch of tartaric acid) Put into a covered jar. Will keep well.

Mr. THOMAS HILL,
12 Gladstone Road, Seacombe.

LEMON SNOW.

12 oz. fine sugar		4 lemons
1 oz. Cox's gelatine		1 pint water
	Whites of 4 eggs	

Put the gelatine in a pan, with 1 pint of water, and let it dissolve very slowly. When quite dissolved add the sugar; stir till the sugar is quite dissolved in the liquid. Strain off into a large basin, and allow to stand till cool, but it must not set. Now add the whites of the four eggs, and the juice of the lemons to the liquid, and beat the whole till quite white and stiff. Pour into glass dishes, and leave to set.

MAIRI NIC'LLE MHUNADH,
A' Choille Bheag, Oban.

LEMON SOLID.

| ½ lb. castor sugar | Juice and rind of 2 lemons |
| ½ gill sherry | 1 pint thick cream |

Stir all but the cream on the stove till the sugar is melted, grating in the lemon rind, then put into a glass dish. Take the cream scalding hot, and holding it up high, pour it over the dish.

To be made the day before it is required.

Mrs. CHARLES BRUCE, 13 Chapel Street, London.

LEMON SOUFFLÉ (cold).

3 eggs	½ lb. sifted sugar
3 lemons	½ oz. gelatine
½ pint cream	

Grate the lemon rind, then squeeze in the juice ; add yolks of eggs, put into a basin in a pan of hot water, till it nearly boils, then let it cook. Whip whites, also cream and sugar. Mix all together, put into a mould or soufflé case to set, and turn out. It should be *very* light.

Miss HUGHES.

LEMON SOUFFLÉ.

| 2 oz. fresh butter | 2 lemons |
| 2 oz. sugar | 4 eggs |

Put the butter, sugar, juice of the two lemons and grated rind of one, and the four yolks, beaten, all into a saucepan, and stir on the fire till it is the consistency of thick cream, but on no account allow the mixture to boil. Then add the whites beaten to a stiff froth, and steam for 16 minutes. When cold and to be served cover the soufflé with cream that is slightly beaten, and ornament to taste.

Miss CAMPBELL of Jura.

LEMON SPONGE.

| ½ oz. gelatine | | 1 pint water |
| 3 oz. lump sugar | | White of 1 egg |

Juice and rind of 3 lemons

Peel the lemon rind (very thinly so as to take only the yellow and *none* of the white) on to the sugar, add the gelatine and *boiling* water ; strain, whip the egg separately for 10 minutes or so, add to other ingredients, and whip all together for three quarters of an hour. This makes a beautifully light sponge.

Miss HUGHES, Beechwood.

LOUISE PUDDING.

| 2 oz. flour | | 1 oz. castor sugar |
| 1 oz. butter | | 3 eggs |

Not quite ½ pint of milk

Stir all but the eggs over the fire quickly till thick and slightly creamy looking, then flavour with vanilla ; when cool add the yolks, and then add *very* lightly the stiffly-whipped white of eggs. Put in a well-buttered mould. Steam gently for an hour (be sure it does not boil).

SAUCE.—2 yolks of eggs, a little sugar and sherry, stir till it thickens, pour all over pudding. It may be coloured pink.

MARMALADE PUDDING.

2 eggs, 2 oz. flour		1 tablespoonful of marmalade
2 oz. butter		Not quite a teaspoonful bicar-
2 oz. castor sugar		bonate of soda

The whites must be whipped and added last, after adding them continue to whip up till quite spongy ; this makes all the difference to the lightness of the pudding. Steam one hour.

Mrs. BEVAN, 18 Sloane Court, London.

MERINGUES.

Whites of 2 eggs, ¼ lb. pounded (*not* sifted) lump sugar.

(Makes about six.)

Beat up the whites on a plate with a knife till they are so stiff as to bear the weight of the knife blade. Put in the sugar very slowly, stirring carefully with the knife, take up the mixture in a wooden spoon, and lay each

spoonful carefully about an inch apart on the oven tin or
a board which has been covered with cap paper. Bake
in a moderate oven till they are a light brown.

Mrs. CAMPBELL of Inverneill.

MILANESE SOUFFLÉ (for 10 people).

½ lb. castor sugar
2¼ lemons
3 eggs
A little grated chocolate (*optional* apricot jam, ratafias, rosepetals)

½ pint cream
½ oz. gelatine
½ gill water

Put the yolks of eggs, sugar, grated lemon rinds (*only* the *yellow*
outer skin) and juice, and two tablespoonfuls water in saucepan,
whisk steadily till nearly boiling (7 minutes), then strain into a
basin and let it get cold. Stir the remaining water and gelatine
over cool part of stove till melted, in separate pan. Stir the
cream (previously whipped) into the egg mixture (*a*), strain in
the gelatine, and lastly, add the lightly whipped white of eggs (*b*).
Let it set creamily, then pour into soufflé mould (round which
a band of paper has been tied, coming 2½ inches above it),
shake it to make it settle down evenly. When set, take off
paper and grate over it the chocolate, and rosepetals and grated
ratafia if liked.

It makes the soufflé lighter and nicer to do as follows :—

Keep back a cupful of mixture (*a*) (*i.e.*, before adding gelatine) pour only half of mixture (*b*) into mould, adding the other
half to the cupful without the gelatine, and also 1 more whipped
white of egg. Put a layer of apricot jam over the mixture in
mould, and add what you kept back (which will be much
lighter) on top and grate on the chocolate. The 4th white of egg
can of course be whipped with the others and kept back. If
vanilla is used instead of lemon, add another ¼ gill of water.

Be sure to use a wooden spoon and not an iron one when
working the lemon mixture.

Miss HUGHES, Beechwood.

MINCE MEAT. 1.

3 lbs. beef suet chopped fine and free from skin. 3 lbs. apples
pared and chopped. 3 lbs. raisins (Valencia) stoned and
chopped. 3 lbs. currants, well cleaned. 3 lbs. brown sugar.
6 lemons, the rind grated, and the juice. 2 oz. citron chopped.
¼ lb. Valencia almonds (or Jordan ditto) blanched and chopped,

the two latter ingredients not to be chopped so fine as the others. 1 teacupful brandy. Mix all together in a stone jar.

Mrs. CAMPBELL of Inverneill.

MINCE MEAT. 2.

1 lb. beef suet, chopped as fine as possible ; 1 lb. raisins, picked, stoned and chopped very fine ; a little allspice ; 1 lb. currants, washed, dried, and stoned ; 1 lb. apples, chopped fine ; 1 lb. brown sugar ; juice of 3 lemons ; $\frac{1}{2}$ nutmeg, grated ; 2 oz. candied peel, 1 oz. candied citron—both chopped fine ; $\frac{1}{2}$ pint brandy.

BEECHWOOD.

MOUSSELINE PUDDING.

4 eggs		2 oz. butter
2 oz. castor sugar		Juice and rind of 1 lemon
	A little cream	

Put the yolks, sugar, butter, lemon and cream in a stewpan, and stir over the fire until nicely thickened ; let this remain until quite cold, then whip the whites of eggs to a stiff froth and add them. Steam in a basin or mould for 1 hour, and serve with whipped cream.

BASHLEY.

MUFFIN PUDDING.

(To use up stale muffins.)

Cut up the muffins (tea-cakes) in slices and steep in wine. Place them alternately with apricot preserve and custard in layers one over the other, till the shape is filled. Steam it through, turn it out on a dish, and serve with wine and arrowroot sauce.

BEECHWOOD.

MUFFIN PUDDING.

4 muffins		$\frac{1}{2}$ lb. dried cherries
1$\frac{1}{2}$ pints milk		A piece of lemon peel
1 wineglassful brandy		Sugar to taste
6 eggs		A little nutmeg
2$\frac{1}{2}$ oz. sweet almonds		Puff paste

Boil the milk with the lemon and loaf sugar for 10 or 12 minutes, then pour it over the muffins. When cold, add the cherries, brandy, almonds (blanched and pounded), and the eggs, well beaten. Mix all these well together, and either boil in a basin or bake in a dish lined with puff paste. Time, 1 hour.

Miss REED, Horsham.

MUSHROOM MERINGUES.

" A PRETTY DISH."

Make some stiff meringue mixture in the usual way. Rub over a baking sheet with white wax or a very little salad oil, and dust with castor sugar. Force the mixture through a forcing back and plain pipe (about ½ inch in diameter) on to the sheet, in rounds about the size of the top of a mushroom ; make some smaller pieces for the stalks, using a smaller pipe. Dust over with icing sugar, and bake immediately in a cool oven for 2 or 3 hours. When they are quite dry and crisp, make a small hole in the centre of the larger pieces on the flat side, lightly brush over with white of egg and dip in grated chocolate. Stick the stalk in the small hole with white of egg or royal icing. Put them in the oven or sun to dry.

Dish up on a bed of whipped cream flavoured with vanilla. Garnish with maidenhair fern.

Miss S. PILKINGTON, Sandside.

NEAPOLITAN PUDDING.

½ a round sponge cake
1 white of egg
2 tablespoonfuls of castor sugar
1 glassful of sherry

½ pint of cream
2 tablespoonfuls of strawberry jam
1 oz. glacé cherries

Cut a thick slice from a round sponge cake ; beat the white of egg till stiff, with a tablespoonful of sugar, and pile it in little heaps all the way round the sponge cake. Bake the cake in a slow oven till the meringue is crisp, and a light brown colour. Take from the oven and pour over a glass of sherry, taking care not to touch the meringue. Have ready the cream (whipped), the crumbs of 2 penny sponge cakes, and 2 tablespoonfuls of strawberry jam. Mix together and pile in the middle of the cake. Scatter chopped glacé cherries over, and serve cold.

Miss Hughes.

NOTTINGHAM PUDDING.

6 large apples		2 oz. of sugar
	1 pint of batter	

Peel the apples and take out the core, and fill them up with sugar; put them in a pie dish, cover them with batter and bake 1 hour.

Miss Reed, Horsham.

OMELETTE AUX POMMES.

Butter, the size of an egg		4 apples
Sugar (brown or white)		6 eggs
	4 teaspoonfuls rum	

Peel and core the apples, cut them into small slices and fry in the butter till the apple is quite tender. Beat the whites and yolks of egg together and pour over the apples; cook, and before rolling it, powder with sugar; then roll, put on a dish and powder again with sugar, burn with a salamander or red hot poker till the sugar becomes caramel. Set on fire the rum, and pour over the omelet. Serve very hot.

Châlet Fairlie, Pau.

FLUFFY OMELET (for 2 persons).

3 eggs, ½ oz. of butter, seasoning.

Beat yolks slightly, add pepper and salt, beat the whites stiffly and add lightly to yolks; melt butter in frying-pan and cook all over a brisk fire, holding pan *before fire* from time to time to cook the top. Go round the edge of the pan with a fork to prevent it sticking. Turn over double when done. If chopped parsley or tongue is used add with the whites. Jam must not be added till after it is cooked. It takes about five minutes.

Miss Hughes.

Folklore and Mythology Archive

OMELETTE SOUFFLÉ PUDDING
(for 2 people).

3 eggs		A pinch of salt
2 oz. white sugar		1 tablespoonful of flour
	Flavouring	

Break the yolks on to the sugar in a basin, beat up well for five minutes, then mix well with it the flour and about a teaspoonful of flavouring (say vanilla essence). Break the whites into a copper or brass pan, add a pinch of salt, and whisk up well till firm enough to bear a half-crown. Whisk slowly at first, getting gradually very quick, it should take about five minutes. Then add to the whites the other mixture in spoonfuls (but by *cutting*, not *stirring*) with a large spoon. Put it on a dish, and sprinkle well with pounded sugar. Bake for 20 minutes in a cool or slow oven.

Miss GRAHAM, Sen., 20 Allan Park, Stirling.

ORANGE CHARLOTTE.

Third of a cupful of cold water		Juice of half a lemon
¼ packet of gelatine		6 oz. castor sugar
Juice of 2 and pulp of 1 or		2 breakfast-cupfuls swiftly
more ordinary oranges		beaten cream
	Some blood oranges	

Dissolve the gelatine in the water slowly, then place in a saucepan on fire, and when melted remove and strain into it the juice and mashed pulp of the yellow oranges, so as to make about a breakfast-cupful in all. Add the strained lemon juice and sugar, mix all well together and set aside to cool. When just about to set fold in the cream. Have ready a mould lined with thin slices of blood oranges, pour in the mixture and place in a cool place till firm. Turn out and serve.

Mrs. BRODRICK.

ORANGE PUDDING.

Butter, the size of a walnut		Rind and juice of 2 oranges
5 yolks of eggs		Lump sugar to taste
	Puff paste	

Put the butter into a stewpan, break into it the yolks of eggs, then grate the rind of two oranges into it, squeeze the juice through a sieve to catch the seeds and pulp; add

as much lump sugar as will make it pleasant, the quantity
depending on the acidity of the oranges, and stir over the
fire till it becomes as thick as custard. Line a dish with
puff paste, put in the orange custard and bake it twenty
minutes.

Miss REED, Horsham.

ORANGE SOUFFLÉ (for 5 or 6 people).

5 eggs	2½ oz. butter
2½ oz. castor sugar	A little cream
Rind of 2 and juice of 1½ oranges	

Put all but the whites of eggs into a pan and stir over the
fire till it thickens, but don't let it boil; then stand it
away for one hour until it gets cold; beat up the whites
of eggs to a stiff froth and add very gently. Bake in a
moderate oven from 3 to 5 minutes.

Miss N. ALEXANDER, The Manor House, Fyfield.

ORANGE TART.

The grated rind of 1 and pulp of 2 Seville oranges	Whites of 3 eggs
Double the weight of this in lump sugar	Pastry
	Pounded sugar

Boil the oranges and lump sugar till nearly as stiff as
marmalade, bake in a paste, the same as for an open tart.
Let it stand till cold. Beat the whites to a stiff froth,
and place them over the tart. Strew pounded sugar
over it and put into the oven till it browns, and send up
hot. About 20 minutes should bake it in rather a slow
oven.

Mrs. CAMPBELL of Inverneill.

PAIN PERDU (for 4 or 5 persons).

3 eggs	Some fresh lard (neither
6 oz. brown sugar	butter nor dripping
8 pieces of bread	will do)

Cut the bread in pieces as if for toast, about 4 inches
long and 2 or 3 inches broad, and not too thick. Mix
eggs and sugar together, and soak the pieces of bread
well both sides in this mixture for 5 minutes or more.

Have ready some *boiling* fresh lard, and into this put the pieces of bread spread out one by one, scrape up the remaining sugar and egg mixture and lay it over the different pieces, fry a light brown and serve hot.

PANCAKES.

6 large tablespoonfuls of flour	½ pint milk
3 eggs	A little salt

As much dripping as would lie on a shilling (or the size of a small nut)

Beat well together the flour, milk, yolks of eggs and salt, then whisk the whites to a *firm froth* and stir well into the mixture. About two minutes before frying put the dripping in the pan and when melted pour in about three parts of an ordinary teacupful of the batter and fry brown on one side, then toss up and fry the other side.

Mrs. CHAS. BRUCE, 13 Chapel Street, London.

ICED PEACH BASKET.

1 lb. bottled peaches	½ wineglassful of maraschino
Sugar	½ pint whipped cream
½ pint cool but liquid lemon jelly	Angelica
(made with ½ oz. of gelatine)	Dried walnuts

Pink colouring

Stew the peaches with a little of the syrup in which they were preserved and sufficient sugar to sweeten them until they are quite soft; then pass them through a sieve and add the lemon jelly, maraschino and cream; colour the mixture a delicate pink, pour into an open mould and place it in an ice case (or in a deep bowl surrounded by broken ice and salt) until it is firm and partially frozen. Then turn it out of the mould, decorate with pieces of angelica, cut into fancy shapes, insert a long piece of angelica in the form of a handle, and fill the middle of the basket with the walnuts, cut into small pieces, and dress with whipped cream.

Miss A. PENNIFOLD,
32 Old Queen Street, London, S.W.

A MOULD OF PEARS.

6 large pears	Quarter of a pint raisin wine
1 pint water	¾ oz. French gelatine
6 cloves	A piece of lemon peel
2 ozs. castor sugar	Juice of half a lemon

Peel and cut into quarters the pears, put them into a pan

with the water, cloves and sugar. Cover the pan over, and put it in the oven till the pears are quite tender. Dip a plain mould in cold water, and when the pears are done place them in the mould. Put into a pan half a pint of the juice from the pears, the raisin wine, lemon peel, lemon juice and gelatine. Let all simmer for six or eight minutes, then strain the liquid over the pears and allow it to cool.

Miss HUGHES.

PLUM PUDDING.

1 lb. suet, chopped very fine	2 oz. candied peel
1 lb. raisins, picked and chopped fine	¾ lb. brown sugar
1 lb. currants, washed, and dried before the fire	1 nutmeg, grated
	Some mixed spice
1 lb. breadcrumbs	1 tablespoonful flour
	8 eggs

Mix well all ingredients except the eggs, beat these for half-an-hour, then add to the rest. Prepare it the night before, and boil it for 10 hours in a mould or basin, and when more water is required you must add boiling water.

Miss E. WILLIAMS.

POMMES À LA DAUPHINE.

2 lb. apples	3 or 4 macaroons
A spoonful of cognac	Thick cream
A piece of cinnamon	A little sugar
Jam	Candied peel

Vanilla flavouring

Peel and take out the cores of the apples, taking care to keep them whole; put them into a stewpan buttered at the bottom, with a very little water, the cinnamon, cognac and sugar. Put the saucepan on a gentle fire to keep them whole, when cooked take them off the fire and place them in a dish or mould. Put into each apple an apricot or some other jam and a small piece of candied peel. Powder the macaroons and sprinkle over the apples. Then pour over sufficient thick cream, flavoured with vanilla, to cover the apples. This dish is perfection if iced.

Miss GRAHAM, Sen., 20 Allan Park, Stirling.

POTATO PUDDING.

1 lb. old potatoes boiled and mashed	3 eggs
2 oz. butter	¼ lb. sugar
1 dozen sweet almonds	1 spoonful cream

Mix well and bake 1 hour. A glass of either brandy or sherry may be added.

BEECHWOOD.

SWEET POTATO SOUFFLÉ.

3 oz. potatoes (boiled, and put through hair or wire sieve)	3 eggs
3 oz. castor sugar	Juice of 2 lemons
	3 oz. butter

Jam or apple purée

Put the potatoes, lemon, sugar, and butter into a basin and whip them together with a fork till it comes to a cream. Take the yolks of the eggs, stir them in with the other things. Butter a dish (soufflé), and put all the ingredients into it. Bake in the oven for 10 minutes. Take it out and put a layer of jam or apples on the top. Whip the whites of the eggs with some castor sugar until it is stiff. Place it on the top and put it in the oven till it comes to a nice brown.

MRS. CHARLES BRUCE.

LITTLE PUDDINGS À LA GRANDE BELLE.

Pistachio nut	3 eggs
Mixed peel	½ pint single cream
Freshly-made brown bread-crumbs	1 tablespoonful maraschino syrup
	1½ oz. castor sugar

Apple purée

Prepare small dariole moulds by buttering with cold butter, sprinkling the bottom with shredded pistachio nuts, and the sides with little shreds of mixed peel. Partly fill the moulds with brown breadcrumbs, then with a custard made of the eggs, cream, maraschino and sugar. Stand the moulds in a saucepan, with a piece of paper beneath them, and add boiling water to about three-parts their weight ; watch the water reboil, then draw the pan to the side and steam ¾ hour. Turn out and serve hot or cold, with an apple purée round.

MISS REED.

LIGHT STEAMED PUDDING.

2 oz. butter
Peel of 2 and juice of 1 lemon

5 eggs

2 oz. castor sugar
2 oz. flour

Chop the lemon peel very fine, work up with the butter to a cream, then add the sugar, work well, then the flour very gently, the yolks of eggs, the lemon juice, and add last the whites of eggs, whipped very stiff. Steam for 80 minutes.

Miss A. PENNIFOLD,
32 Old Queen Street, Westminster.

PUDDING À LA ST. GEORGE.

¼ lb. of butter
Rind of 1 lemon (chopped fine)
¼ lb. of castor sugar
5 oz. of sponge or vanilla biscuit crumbs
1 oz. of fine sifted flour

3 eggs
4 oz. of beef suet
¼ wineglassful of brandy
3 apricots and pistachio nuts
1 oz. of dried cherries

Put the butter and lemon peel into a basin and work till it is a cream, then add the sugar and work for 5 minutes, then the biscuit crumbs and the flour; work these 5 minutes, and add by degrees the yolks of eggs and the finely-chopped suet, the brandy, the apricots cut up in fine slices, and the whites of eggs slightly whipped. Have ready a mould, well buttered, ornamented with dried cherries, apricots, and blanched and shredded pistachio nuts, then put in the prepared mixture and steam for 2½ hours.

Miss REED, Horsham.

PRINCESS PUDDING.

4 eggs
2 tablespoonfuls apricot jam

3 leaves of gelatine
½ pint cream

Whip the eggs and jam in an egg bowl over a slow fire until they present the appearance of thick batter. Then add the gelatine and (whipped) cream; then put in a charlotte mould. Serve with apricot sauce.

Mrs. W. E. CRUM, Fyfield.

PUDDING À LA PRINCESSE.

¼ lb. butter
¼ lb. sugar
2½-oz. breadcrumbs, soaked
  in boiled milk

Rind and juice of 1 lemon
Chopped citron
Apricot sauce
2 eggs

Mix the butter and sugar to a cream, adding the 2 eggs (one at a time) and other ingredients. Line the mould with chopped citron, steam for 1 hour, and serve with apricot sauce.

Miss A. Pennifold,

32 Old Queen Street, Westminster.

PRINCESS PUDDING (cold).

6 eggs
6 oz. sugar
¾ oz. gelatine

1 glassful sherry
¼ glassful maraschino
Juice of 1 lemon

Beat up all but the whites of egg, then beat over hot water for 10 minutes, take off, beat until cold, then add the well-beaten whites of egg; put into mould and serve with sweet sauce.

Mrs. Ellison,

The Vicarage, Windsor.

PUFF PASTRY.

1¼ lb. flour   1¼ lb. butter

Let the flour be quite dry, put it in a small basin. Cut the butter into small pieces, cover it well with the flour in the basin, add salt, add only sufficient water to pick up the flour, roll it as seldom as possible and always the same way; do not roll hard; fold it up and roll it only about 4 times, till it blisters a little.

Mrs. Campbell of Inverneill.

PUFF PASTE.

½ lb. flour   ½ lb. butter (fresh if possible)
Rather less than ½ gill water
(The butter must be *hard*. Stand it on ice if soft.)

Rub flour (all except a large handful) and not quite half the butter between fingers of both hands *lightly*, till a handful of it will press together just like dough, and there are no lumps; then mix in the water with a knife till it sticks. Then roll it out on the board (always in the same direction, if possible); take a third of the remaining butter and press little bits of it into the dough till evenly covered, sprinkle with flour, fold over the ends so that they overlap, sprinkle again, turn half round so that what were the ends become the sides (folded side always uppermost), roll out (away from you), spread on another third of the butter, repeat operations as before, then the remaining third and repeat the folding and rolling. Leave folded up till required, when roll out and cut to size required. It is better if kept for an hour or two.

For French pastry cut it into strips one-eighth of an inch in width, and lay on a baking tin, one inch apart. Cook for $\frac{1}{4}$ of an hour in brisk oven.

For medium puff paste use 1 lb. flour, 12 oz. butter, about 1 gill water.

PRUNE PUDDING.

7 oz. breadcrumbs	1 teacupful of moist sugar
6 oz. suet	1 glass of rum or wine
$\frac{1}{2}$ lb. of prunes	5 or 6 eggs

Cut the prunes in two and take out the stones and kernels, mix them with the other ingredients. Put all in a shape, cover with a floured cloth and boil three hours.

Mrs. W. E. CRUM.

PRUNE SHAPE.

1 lb. prunes	The rind of 1 and the juice of
$\frac{3}{4}$ oz. gelatine	2 lemons
$1\frac{1}{2}$ gills of water	2 ozs. of lump sugar
$\frac{1}{2}$ teaspoonful of cochineal	

Wash the prunes in cold water, place them in a saucepan with the lemon rind and cover with cold water, bring them slowly to the boil, then simmer gently on the side of the stove for one hour. Put them on to a dish and remove the stones. Put the syrup, sugar, gelatine, juice of lemons and cochineal, and stones from the prunes into a pan by the side of the fire for 8 or 10 minutes until the gelatine is thoroughly melted, stirring occasionally. Place the prunes in a mould, strain the syrup, pour over prunes, and put into a cool place till wanted. Turn out into a glass dish and serve with whipped cream or custard.

Miss HUGHES.

QUICKLY-MADE PUDDING.

¼ lb. butter	1 pint milk
¼ lb. sifted sugar	Yolks of 5 eggs and whites of 3
¼ lb. flour	A little grated lemon rind

Make the milk hot, stir in the butter and let it cool; then stir in the sugar, flour and eggs, well whisked; flavour with the lemon rind, and beat the mixture well. Butter some small cups and rather more than half fill them. Bake from 20 minutes to half-an-hour, and serve with custard or wine sauce.

Miss REED, Horsham.

QUANSIONS PUDDING.

½ oz. of isinglass	Sugar
1 pint of milk	Jam
Yolks of 3 eggs	¼ pint of cream
Grated chocolate	

Dissolve the isinglass in the milk, beat up the yolks of eggs and pour the boiling milk on them, add sugar to taste, and set it to cool; when just upon setting whip up ¼ pint of cream and add it to the custard. Whip all together and put it into a small soufflé dish, with a layer of jam at the bottom. Just before serving it whip up some cream, put it on the top and sift a little grated chocolate over, also a little pounded sugar.

Mrs. CARRIE EARLE.

RASPBERRY PUDDING.

Weight of 3 eggs in butter and flour	3 tablespoonfuls raspberry or other jam
Weight of 2 eggs in sugar	1 teaspoonful bicarbonate of soda

Beat the butter to a cream, add sugar, flour and jam, also egg, well beaten, and soda. Beat all together for 10 minutes, put in bowl or mould and boil for 4½ hours. Serve with or without sauce.

Mrs. F. BATESON, Bell Farm, Clewer.

RASPBERRY SHAPE.

Boil a good cupful of small sago in one pint of water, add one pot raspberry jam, stir well together. Pour into mould, and serve with custard sauce.

Mrs. ELLISON, The Vicarage, Windsor.

RATAFIA OR SCALDED CREAM.

3 or 4 bay, peach or nectarine leaves	Yolks of 3 eggs
1 pint of cream	Sugar to taste
	A large spoonful of brandy

Boil 3 or 4 bay, peach or nectarine leaves in a full pint of cream, strain it, and when cold add the yolks of eggs beaten and strained, sugar and brandy stirred quickly into it. Scald till thick, stirring it all the time.

Mrs. W. E. CRUM.

RED GROUT.

3½ lbs. juice of currants	½ oz. minced bitter almonds
3 pints of water	1 lb. sago
1 oz. minced sweet almonds	1 oz. pounded cinnamon
Sugar to taste	

Put all, except the sago, together in a pot on the fire, and when it begins to boil add the sago (first rinsing it well in cold water). Now boil for a quarter of an hour, stirring frequently. Wet (with cold water) cups or shapes inside, fill them, and let it stand to cool. Turn out on to a dish, and serve with cream and sugar.

BEECHWOOD.

RHUBARB SHAPE.

1 lb. pink rhubarb, peeled	2 tablespoonfuls water
¾ lb. sugar	Grated rind of a lemon

Boil all together for 20 minutes, then strain the juice from the rhubarb and boil the juice for half-an-hour, then all together again and put into a mould.

BEECHWOOD.

ROYAL COBURG PUDDING.

1 pint new milk		6 oz. currants
6 oz. flour		6 oz. sugar
6 oz. butter		6 eggs

A little nutmeg and brandy to taste

Mix the flour to a smooth batter with milk, add the remaining ingredients gradually, and when well mixed half-fill your basins or moulds. Bake three-quarters of an hour. Turn out the puddings on a dish, and serve with wine.

Miss REED, Horsham.

SAGO SOUFFLÉ.

3 tablespoonfuls sago		3 oz. sugar
1½ gills milk		Yolks of 4 and whites of 6 eggs

Soak sago in sugar and milk two hours or more, beat yolks and whites to a stiff froth and mix with sago. Bake from 25 minutes to half-an-hour in a slow oven.

Miss HUGHES, Beechwood.

SANDWICH PASTRY.

¼ lb. butter		¼ lb. flour
¼ lb. sugar		3 eggs

¼ teaspoonful baking powder

Cream butter and sugar, add eggs and flour, and the baking powder last of all. Bake in a moderate oven for half-an-hour.

Miss A. PENNIFOLD,
32 Old Queen Street, Westminster.

SPANISH PUFFS.

Rind of 1 lemon or orange		2 oz. of fresh butter
¼ pint of milk		3 oz. of flour
4 eggs		A dessertspoonful of sugar

Bring milk to a boil, add butter and sugar and the rind of lemon or orange grated fine; stir flour in very quickly till it leaves the side of the saucepan clean; it must be free from lumps. Take off the fire, let it stand till the heat has gone, then break in 4 yolks of eggs, one at a time, beat the whites to a stiff froth and add to the other ingredients. Let it stand for two hours. Beat well, and then fry in hot lard from 10 to 15 minutes. It should be the size of an egg when fried. Serve with fruit syrup.

Miss WALDER, Horsham.

SNOW CHEESE.

| 1 pint cream | Wineglassful sherry |
| Juice of 2 lemons | Sugar to taste |

Add the lemon juice to the cream, also the sherry and sugar, beat up till quite thick, put on a cloth which may have been placed on the frame of a small sieve, of which the bottom has been taken out, and let it drain till morning.

Mrs. CAMPBELL of Inverneill.

SPANISH PUDDING.

6 oz. raisins	6 oz. suet
6 oz. carrots	6 eggs
6 oz. currants	3 oz. sugar
6 oz. potatoes	A little salt and nutmeg

Mix all together, put into a buttered mould and boil for 6 or 8 hours.

Miss A. PENNIFOLD,
32 Old Queen Street, Westminster.

STONE CREAM.

| 1 lemon | ½ oz. isinglass, sugar to taste |
| 1 pint cream | Preserved apricots or plums |

Squeeze the juice of the lemon into a glass dish, grate the rind, then lay upon it the fruit, have ready the cream with the isinglass dissolved in it, sweeten this and let it be *nearly* cold before you pour it over the fruit.

Mrs. CAMPBELL of Inverneill.

SMALL SUET PUDDING.

2 very full tablespoonfuls *very*	3 very full tablespoonfuls
finely chopped mutton or	flour
beef suet	½ an egg (white and yolk)
A pinch of salt	mixed in ¼ pint milk
A little baking powder	

Beat all together till it is a thick batter. Boil quite an hour in a very small basin.

Mrs. PITT-TAYLOR.

SULTANA PUDDING.

5 oz. suet		5 oz. sultanas
5 oz. flour		A little milk
	2 dessert-spoonfuls treacle	

Mix all together and boil for 5 hours.

Miss A. PENNIFOLD,
32 Old Queen Street, Westminster.

TANGERINE ICE.

6 Tangerine oranges		½ lemon
2 ordinary oranges		Syrup

Squeeze the juice of the oranges and lemon into a basin, then add sufficient syrup (flavoured with the peel of the two oranges and a *little* lemon peel) to sweeten; let it stand for 4 or 5 hours, then strain and freeze; put it back into the skins and serve.

Miss A. PENNIFOLD,
32 Old Queen Street, Westminster.

TAPIOCA BLANC MANGE.

1 pint of milk		4 sweet and 4 bitter ⎱ pounded
½ pint of cream		almonds ⎰ together
2 oz. of tapioca		3 lumps of sugar
	½ oz. of gelatine	

Soak the tapioca in a little water from 1 to 2 hours till it is soft, and soak the gelatine 10 to 15 minutes. Boil the milk and cream with the sugar and almonds for 10 minutes, then pour it over the prepared tapioca. Stir this round a few times, put it back into the saucepan, add the gelatine, and let all simmer till both tapioca and gelatine are dissolved; remove from the fire, stir till cool, then pour into a wet mould.

Miss REED.

TAPIOCA CREAM.

Steep some tapioca in milk for 3 hours, then cover it, and let it simmer slowly on the fire till it is well cooked. Then turn it out and let it stand till cold. Have some cream, seasoned and whipped up rather stiff; add it to the tapioca, and whip together for a few minutes.

Mrs. W. E. CRUM.

Historic Cookbooks of the World

STEAMED TAPIOCA PUDDING.

2 oz. French tapioca	¾ pint of milk
Sugar to taste	3 eggs

Put the tapioca and milk into a stewpan, place it on the side of the stove to cook slowly ; when cooked add 3 eggs, the yolks and whites separately, the whites whipped very stiff ; add sugar to taste, and steam very slowly for 1½ hours.

Serve with mousseline sauce.

Mousseline Sauce for Pudding.

2 yolks of eggs	Sugar
1 gill of cream	Flavouring

Take the yolks of eggs, cream and a little sugar ; put it all into a stewpan, and stand the stewpan in another stewpan that has some boiling water in it. Well whip till it thickens, being careful the sauce does not curdle. Flavour with a little maraschino or other flavouring.

Miss A. PENNIFOLD,

32 Old Queen Street, Westminster.

TRANSPARENT PUDDING.

4 yolks of eggs	¼ lb. butter
¼ lb. sugar	

Melt sugar and butter in a basin in the oven, then, when not too hot, put the eggs to them. Fill a shape and steam for 2 hours.

BEECHWOOD.

TREACLE SPONGE.

¼ lb. flour	A pinch of salt
¼ lb. suet	1 teaspoonful ground ginger
½ teaspoonful carbonate of soda	1 oz. treacle
	1 gill milk
1 egg	

Mix well together and boil for 2 hours. Pour some hot golden syrup round the dish.

Half this quantity makes a good-sized pudding.

Miss YEATMAN.

TRIFLE.

(A specially good old recipe, with froth as light as snow.)

Spongecakes	Some good thick custard
Raspberry or strawberry jam	1 quart milk
2 wineglassfuls sherry	1 pint cream

It takes 3 days to make.

Cover the bottom of the dish with spongecakes spread with jam, pour over them the wine and custard, and let it stand for two days. The froth must stand 7 hours on the sieve before it is wanted, and is made as follows:—

FROTH.—Put the cream into a basin and some of the milk to it, and beat it up to a froth; lift up the froth with a spoon and place it on a sieve, and place the sieve over a flat dish. Keep on adding milk by degrees to the cream to make more froth. What milk runs from the froth on to the dish must be put back to the basin of cream. It will take nearly 2 sieves *full* of froth to make the trifle look nice.

Miss ELLEN WILLIAMS.

VANILLA CREAM.

1 oz. gelatine	½ pint milk
¼ pint water	1½ tablespoonfuls castor sugar
3 eggs	1 teaspoonful vanilla essence
½ pint whipped cream	

Soak the gelatine in the water, make a custard of the eggs, milk and sugar, then add the vanilla essence. Dissolve the gelatine in a small pan and strain into the custard. When the custard is cool mix with the whipped cream, and put into the mould just before the custard begins to set.

Mrs. BRODRICK.

STEAMED VANILLA SOUFFLE.

1 oz. of flour	1 gill of milk
1 oz. of butter	2 eggs
A little sugar	Flavouring

Melt butter in a saucepan, dredge in the flour, add milk and stir till it thickens, take off the fire, add flavouring, sugar, yolks of eggs and whites, which have been beaten to a stiff froth; put into a well-greased soufflé dish and steam 20 or 30 minutes. Pour fruit juice round for a sauce.

Miss REED.

VANILLA SOUFFLÉ.

1½ oz. butter	3 oz. castor sugar
1 oz. flour	1½ gills milk
Yolks of 3 and whites of	Small teaspoonful vanilla
4 or 5 eggs	essence

Stir butter, flour, sugar, and milk and yolks rapidly over fire with wooden spoon from 3 to 5 minutes, till it is a good thick smooth batter, or you may add the yolks after it is cooked. Leave it to cool (it will not hurt it to stand all day); just before baking add the vanilla and stiffly-whipped whites; mix well (bubbles should rise to the surface); pour into china soufflé dish (round which a band of buttered paper has been tied), and bake from 20 minutes to half an hour. The success of the soufflé depends on the baking. The oven should be rather over moderate heat, so that you can just bear your hand in it. Place the soufflé on a baking tin in the lower half, and 4 or 5 minutes before it is done (when it has risen up to the paper) remove it to the top half of the oven to brown. Rather let the oven get hotter than colder during the cooking, but an even heat is best. The soufflé should be light as a feather, and partly liquid. Do not open the oven door more than twice while cooking.

Miss HUGHES.

WAFER PUDDINGS.

2 oz. flour	2 eggs
1½ oz. butter	A little sugar

¼ pint milk

Beat flour, butter and sugar together; beat the eggs well, add milk and mix all together, pour into buttered saucers and bake a light brown; put jam in the centre and fold, powder with white sugar. They should be very light.

Mrs. BEVAN, 18 Sloane Court, London.

WATER PUDDING.

8 tablespoonfuls of cold water	1 oz. butter
The juice and rind of a lemon	The yolks of 4 eggs and the
½ lb. of sugar	whites beaten to a froth

Mix all well together and bake in a buttered pie dish for an hour in a slow oven.

Mrs. MACDONALD of Dunach.

WINE JELLY.

2 oz. gelatine	3 pints water
1 lb. lump sugar	3½ glasses sherry (and if liked a few
Rind of 5 lemons and juice of 7	drops of brandy)

Whites and shells of 2 eggs

This makes 2 quarts of jelly.

Put the lemon juice and rind, sugar, and gelatine in a saucepan (copper or enamel lined), add 2 pints cold water, and when the gelatine is soft, one pint boiling water. Beat the eggs to a stiff froth with the broken shells, add them to the rest and beat over the fire till it boils, let it simmer 5 minutes. Put it 2 or 3 times through a jelly bag; when nearly cold, but not stiff, add the wine, pour into mould, and place on ice if you have it. (Before putting it through the jelly bag pour boiling water through the latter, but the bag must not be too wet or the jelly will not be firm.)

Miss HUGHES, Beechwood.

ADDITIONAL RECIPES.

ADDITIONAL RECIPES.

Ye Wise Men came from Ye East, but Ye Wise Woman goes to the Yeast,
And the Yeast she will have is the

"D.C.L."

because she knows it is perfect and guaranteed pure. It makes nice sweet bread, buns, tea-cakes, etc., of splendid appearance and tempting flavour. Don't forget to ask for "D.C.L."

Send for Booklet of Instructions to Sole Manufacturers: | **The DISTILLERS CO., Ltd., EDINBURGH.**

CAKES, Etc.

ANGEL CAKE.

Whites of 5 or 6 eggs
2½ oz. flour
1 teaspoonful of vanilla
essence

5 oz. fine sifted sugar
1 small teaspoonful of
cream of tartar

This cake bakes better in small shapes than large. Butter the insides of two small tin shapes, and sprinkle over with sugar. Put the whites in a basin and beat to a perfectly stiff froth. Add all the sugar at once and beat a few minutes longer. Take out the whisk and replace it with a spoon, and sift the flour in mixed with the cream of tartar. Mix it very gently and as little as possible. Add the vanilla, and mix it in. Pour into the shapes, sprinkle a little sugar on the top, and put it into a warm *(not hot)* oven for about half-an-hour.

Mrs. W. E. CRUM.

PURE HOUSEHOLD BREAD.

6 lbs. best flour
1 quart water at 95°

2 oz. malt extract

1 oz. yeast
1 oz. salt

Put flour in a bowl, dissolve yeast, salt, and extract in the water, then add to the flour and make up into a nice firm clear dough. Cover over with a cloth and keep in a warm place for 1 hour, then well knead it and let it stand for another hour, when it is ready for the oven. About 1 hour in oven (500°).

Mr. THOMAS HILL, Baker,
12 Gladstone Road, Seacombe.

STEAMED BROWN BREAD.

1 lb. wheaten meal	½ teaspoonful cream of tartar
1 teaspoonful carbonate of soda	Pinch of salt

Buttermilk

Mix all into a nice dough with buttermilk, and steam for 2 hours in a cake tin.

Mrs. LE CHALLAS, Glenfinart.

BRIDE CAKE.

1 lb. butter	1¼ lb. peel (cut small)
1 lb. sugar	½ oz. spice
1¼ flour	16 eggs
2 lbs. currants	½ pint brandy

Cream thoroughly the butter and sugar ; add eggs, 2 at a time, till the whole is well beaten; then add the remainder of ingredients; mix, and bake in a slow oven for about 4 hours.

"ALMOND PASTE FOR TOP."—½ lb. ground almonds, ¾ lb. fine castor sugar, 2 or 3 drops of orange flower water. Work into a firm paste with 2 or 3 yolks, and cover top of cake.

ICING FOR CAKE.—1 lb. icing sugar, well beaten with whites of egg and 2 or 3 drops of lemon juice, till it will spread smoothly on cake.

Mr. SHONK, Leytonstone.

BOHEMIAN CAKE.

½ lb. butter	6 oz. fine flour
½ lb. castor sugar	¼ lb. peel
2 oz. grated chocolate	½ oz. baking powder
The rind of 1 lemon	3 eggs

Work the butter to a cream, add the sugar, lemon, yolks of eggs, flour, peel, lastly add the whites beaten very stiff. Bake for 45 minutes in moderate oven.

Mrs. ELLISON.

BROOKSBY LUNCHEON CAKE.

1½ lbs. flour	1 good teaspoonful car-
1 lb. sultana raisins	bonate of soda
¾ lb. fresh or salt butter	A pint of buttermilk, or
6 oz. brown sugar	as much as will make
1 oz. nutmeg (grated)	it of a nice consistency

Rub the butter into the flour, mix thoroughly all the dry ingredients, buttermilk last. Bake in a slow oven for 2 hours.

Mrs. GRAHAM of Skipness.

BROWN CAKE.

1 lb. flour	1 teaspoonful baking soda
1 lb. currants	1 teaspoonful cinnamon
½ lb. butter	1 teaspoonful spice
½ lb. sugar	6 eggs

Line a cake-tin with greased paper. Beat butter and sugar to a cream, and sift flour, spices, and baking soda into a basin. Beat the eggs very well. Add to the creamed butter and sugar a little of the egg, then a little flour, beat well; continue adding egg and flour and beating well till all are used up. Then lastly add the fruit, and pour into the cake-tin. Place in a moderate oven, and bake for 1½ hours.

MAIRI NIC'LLE MHUNADH.

A'Choille Bheag, Oban.

RICH LARGE BUNLOAF.

2 lbs. flour	4 to 6 tablespoonfuls brewers'
½ lb. sugar	or German barm (1½d or 2d
½ lb. butter and good drip-	worth)
ping (half of each)	4 eggs
2 breakfast-cupfuls milk	1½ lbs. washed fruits

Mix the flour and sugar, rub into them the butter and dripping, then warm the milk, mix it with the barm, and while still warm pour it into a hole in the middle of the flour, etc., stirring a *little* of the flour, etc., into the liquid. Put before the fire for 1 hour to rise. Beat the eggs well, mix into the cake, then the fruits. Mix well, put in a tin, leave before the fire 1 hour (or 1½ hours if cold weather) to rise again; then bake 1 hour.

Miss E. WILLIAMS, Delfield.

CAKE MIXTURE.

½ lb. butter	A pinch of baking powder
½ lb. sugar	½ lb. sultanas
½ lb. flour	4 eggs
	6 drops vanilla

Mix butter and sugar till creamed. Break in the eggs, one by one, work it with the hand five minutes to each egg. Bake 1½ hours.

Miss S. PILKINGTON of Sandside.

RICH CAKE.

1 lb. butter	½ lb. citron
13 oz. sugar	½ lb. cherries, cut up
1 nutmeg (grated)	1 lb. flour
14 eggs	1 lb. well washed and
1 lb. stoned raisins	dried currants
½ lb. chopped almonds	¾ lb. sultanas

A little essence of almonds

Beat butter to a cream, add sugar and nutmeg, beat well together, add raw yolks of eggs, beat for 10 minutes, add the fruits and almond essence, mix well, and, lastly, add the stiffly-whipped whites and the flour warmed and passed through a sieve. Do not make the cake very deep; rather use 2 tins. Bake 5 hours in a slow oven.

ALMOND ICING.—To 1 lb. finely-chopped almonds add 1½ lb. icing sugar, 3 raw whites of eggs, and a little vanilla essence. Work into a dry stiff paste, and use.

Miss S. PILKINGTON of Sandside.

RICH CURRANT CAKE.

1 lb. butter	1½ lb. candied peel
1 lb. castor sugar	16 eggs
1 lb. flour	A pinch of spice
1½ lb. currants	Quartern of rum or brandy

Well cream together the butter and sugar, adding the eggs one or two at a time (care should be taken to add eggs slowly, to prevent curdling). When it is thoroughly beaten add remainder of ingredients and mix. Bake in a moderate oven two or three hours.

Mr. SHONK.

CHOCOLATE CAKE. 1.

3 eggs	2 oz. flour
¼ lb. butter	2 oz. pounded almonds
¼ lb. castor sugar	6 drops vanilla
3 oz. grated chocolate	Saltspoonful baking powder

Beat butter and sugar well together, add flour, eggs, etc., gradually. Beat 10 minutes, add baking powder, and pour into tin.

FOR THE ICING.—1½ bars chocolate and enough water to make a paste, then add icing sugar. White of egg and icing sugar for decoration.

Mrs. G. FLETCHER.

INEXPENSIVE CHOCOLATE CAKE. 2.

¼ lb. butter	¾ teacupful of milk
6 oz. sifted sugar	8 oz. flour
3 eggs	1 teaspoonful baking powder
6 oz. chocolate	½ teaspoonful of cinnamon (if liked)

1 teaspoonful of vanilla

Beat the butter and sugar to a cream, add the eggs (well beaten), grate the chocolate and dissolve over the fire in the milk, add to the butter, sugar and eggs, then add the flour, baking powder, vanilla and cinnamon. Beat very well. Bake for half-an-hour.

Miss STIRLING, Gargunnock, Stirling.

CHOCOLATE CAKE. 3.

6 oz. butter	3 oz. grated chocolate
6 oz. sugar	3 eggs, beaten separately

6 oz. breadcrumbs

Time, 15 minutes, in a moderate oven. Cut in rounds before it is cool.

ICING.—4 oz. butter, 6 oz. icing sugar, few drops coffee essence, 2 oz. grated chocolate. Spread between the rounds of cake.

Mrs. ELLISON, The Vicarage, Windsor.

RICH CHOCOLATE CAKE. 4.

¼ lb grated chocolate	¾ lb. sifted sugar
½ lb. pounded almonds	8 eggs
2 tablespoonfuls potato flour	Few drops vanilla

Beat yolks of eggs and sugar for 20 minutes, add almonds, chocolate and potato flour, beat whites stiffly and add lightly. Bake slowly.

Miss STIRLING, Gargunnock.

GENOA CAKE.

1 lb. butter	½ lb. glacé cherries, halved
1 lb. castor sugar	½ lb. currants
1¼ lb. flour	½ lb. citron peel
1 lb. sultanas	10 eggs

Thoroughly cream together the butter and sugar, slowly adding the eggs, when thoroughly beaten add other ingredients, and mix. Sprinkle some blanched split almonds on top of cake. Moderate oven, about 1½ hours.

Mr. SHONK, Leytonstone.

GINGER CAKE.

1 lb. flour	3 eggs
½ oz. allspice	½ teaspoonful carbonate
1 oz. ginger	of soda
¾ lb. syrup	½ pint of warm milk
¼ lb. treacle	1 teaspoonful vinegar
¼ lb. butter	½ lb. coarse brown sugar

Put the flour into a basin, add the sugar then the allspice and ginger, mix well; cream the butter, add syrup and treacle; dissolve the carbonate of soda in the milk, then the vinegar; mix all the ingredients together, and the eggs last of all. Pour it on a floured flat tin, and bake in a good oven. Time, half-an-hour.

Mrs. GRAHAM of Skipness.

ORIGINAL ORMSKIRK GINGERBREAD.

1 lb. patent flour	½ oz. ground ginger
6 oz. butter	¼ oz. ground spice
8 oz. moist sugar	A small pinch of ground
2 eggs	caraway seeds

12 oz. syrup

Put butter, sugar, eggs, spices and syrup in bowl, give it a good beating up till quite smooth, then add flour, and make it into a firm dough; this dough must remain at least a week before baking, if a month all the better. When wanted for use take a piece, roll out thick as a penny piece, then with your cutter cut out, place on well-buttered sheet and bake in very cool oven about half-an-hour.

Mr. THOMAS HILL, Baker,
Gladstone Road, Seacombe.

FRUIT GINGERBREAD LOAF.

1 lb. flour	½ oz. spice
¾ lb. syrup	½ oz. ground ginger
¼ lb. lemon peel	1 oz. carbonate of soda
6 oz. butter	1 teacupful sour milk
6 oz. moist sugar	4 eggs

1 lb. sultanas

Warm butter, sugar and syrup in a basin, add all the other ingredients to the flour, and make up, about 12 oz. in each tin. Will take 1½ hours in a very cool oven. On no account touch them till baked, or they will drop in the centre and be spoilt.

Mr. THOMAS HILL, Baker,
Gladstone Road, Seacombe.

GINGERBREAD LOAF.

1 lb. flour
½ lb. butter
½ lb. brown sugar
½ pint treacle
1½ oz. ground caraway

1½ oz. ground cinnamon
¼ teaspoonful mixed spice
¼ lb. candied peel
½ teaspoonful carbonate of soda
½ teaspoonful cream of tartar

3 eggs

Cream butter and sugar together, whisk eggs, whites and yolks together, mix them in; next add treacle, and lastly flour, into which the cream of tartar, soda and seasoning has been mixed. Bake in moderate oven.

Mrs. SMALL of Dirnanean.

GINGERBREAD.

2 lbs. flour
2 lbs. treacle
1 lb. butter
1 lb. raisins
¼ lb. mixed peel

Citron
2 lemons
½ lb. moist sugar
4 oz. ginger
2 teaspoonfuls carbonate of soda

4 eggs

Rub the butter in the flour, warm the treacle, put the soda and eggs into the treacle (beat the eggs first). Bake in rather a quick oven. When the cake is risen let the heat of the oven go down. It takes 1¾ hours to bake. Keep a week before using.

BROADMEADOWS.

GINGER CAKE.

1 lb. sifted flour
½ lb. sugar
¼ lb. butter
½ lb. treacle and syrup mixed, but more of syrup
2 eggs

1 small tablespoonful ginger, cinnamon and allspice
1 small teacupful warm milk
6 oz. raisins
A few almonds, blanched and sliced

Rub the butter into the flour, add all the dry ingredients, beat up the two eggs and mix with treacle and syrup, and mix into the cake; lastly add the warm milk, in which has been dissolved one teaspoonful baking soda, and add the fruit. Pour into two paper-lined cake tins and bake in moderate oven.

ABDEN, Dornoch.

GINGERBREAD.

3 lbs. flour, half of it prepared	A large cupful buttermilk
1 lb. butter	½ lb. currants
1½ lb. sugar	½ lb. sultana raisins
1 lb. syrup	¼ lb. orange peel
10 eggs	¼ lb. green ginger
	2 oz. allspice

Beat butter, sugar, and eggs well; then add all other ingredients.

Mr. JAMES KIRKWOOD, Baker,
Kirklee, Fairlie.

JELLY SANDWICH.

6 oz. flour	¼ lb. sifted sugar
1 oz. Paisley flour	1 egg
2 oz. butter	1 gill milk

Rub butter into flour, then add sugar and egg well beaten, also milk. Butter two round tins, divide mixture between the two, and when ready spread with jelly and put together. Bake in quick oven from 15 to 20 minutes.

Miss M. BLACK, Oronsay, Connell.

LUNCHEON CAKE.

12 oz. flour	2 oz. candied peel
½ lb. butter	¼ lb. sugar
6 oz. currants	Teaspoonful baking powder
6 oz. raisins	
4 eggs	

Mix the butter with the flour, rubbing in well, and add sugar, raisins, etc. Mix the eggs in well (whole) with hands, and put in tin; bake 1½ hours.

Miss S. PILKINGTON, Sandside, Caithness.

MADEIRA CAKE.

½ lb. flour	½ teaspoonful baking powder
6 oz. sifted sugar	Grated rind of ½ a lemon
1 tablespoonful milk	Pinch of salt
6 oz. butter	3 eggs

Sift the flour, beat the eggs well, beat the butter and sugar to a cream, add a little flour, then a little egg, and so on until all is used up. If the mixture seems too stiff add a little milk, then the lemon rind, salt and baking powder.

Pour the mixture into a prepared cake tin. Bake in a moderate oven for about 1½ hours. When the cake is half-baked lay a piece of citron peel on the top.

Miss M. BLACK, Oronsay, Connell.

MADEIRA CAKE.

1 lb. patent flour		18 oz. fresh butter
12 oz. plain flour		18 oz. castor sugar
	12 eggs	

Sieve the flour, put butter and sugar in a bowl and well cream up, adding the eggs 2 at a time, and well beating between. Place your cake rings on a sheet, line them with white paper, sides and bottom, and weigh into them 12 oz. of the cake batter ; now place a very thin slice of citron peel on top and bake in a good oven, taking care that they do not take on too much colour. Will take about 30 minutes. This is a really grand cake, but all depends on well beating up the batter.

Mr. THOMAS HILL.

ORANGE CAKE. 1.

The weight of 2 eggs in flour		1 teaspoonful of baking
and sugar		powder
2 oz. butter		1 orange
	3 tablespoonfuls icing sugar	

Beat the butter and sugar to a cream, then add the rind of the orange grated and half the juice. Then well beat the two eggs, and, last of all, add the baking powder. Bake in a moderate oven for 30 minutes. Pour over the following mixture, while the cake is hot : 3 tablespoonfuls of icing sugar mixed with the juice of half the orange.

Miss A. PENNIFOLD,
32 Old Queen Street, London.

ORANGE CAKE. 2.

2 oz. flour		2 eggs
1½ oz. butter		1 orange
1 small teaspoonful of baking		The weight of two eggs in
powder		sugar

Beat the eggs for 10 minutes, then add the sugar and flour and the butter slightly melted and the grated rind of orange, and beat all well for 6 or 7 minutes, and then add the baking powder and the juice of the orange, and put in a well-greased tin about 2 inches in depth, and cook in a moderate oven for a quarter of an hour.

Miss HUGHES.

ORMIDALE SODA PLUM CAKE.

4 oz. fruit (currants and raisins)	A piece of peel
4 oz. brown sugar	1 teaspoonful soda
4 oz. butter	2 kitchen teacupfuls of milk
8 oz. flour	2 teaspoonfuls mixed spice

Mix soda and spice in the milk. Cream butter and sugar, then add other ingredients. Mince the raisins. Very hot oven required. Mixture must be very moist.

Mrs. BURNLEY CAMPBELL of Ormidale.

SCRIPTURE CAKE.

4½ cupfuls flour	½ cupful milk
1½ cupfuls butter	2 teaspoonfuls honey
2 cupfuls sugar	A pinch of salt
2 cupfuls raisins	2 tablespoonfuls baking powder
2 cupfuls currants	Seasoning of spices
1 cupful almonds	

Beat well together.

Mrs. ELLISON, The Vicarage, Windsor.

PLAIN SEED CAKE.

2 lbs. dough	½ lb. moist sugar
¼ lb. lard	3 eggs

1 tablespoonful caraway seeds

Rub the lard to a cream; beat the whites and yolks of egg separately. Bake in a moderate oven.

Mrs. CAMPBELL of Inverneill.

SPICE CAKE.

1 lb. flour	½ lb. sultanas
½ lb. butter	2 teaspoonfuls baking powder
½ lb. sugar	2 eggs
Teaspoonful spice	

A little milk

Bake 3 hours in a slow oven.

Mrs. W. E. CRUM.

SPONGE CAKE.

4 eggs		6 oz. castor sugar
	4 oz. flour	

Whisk yolks for 7 minutes, whites for 10 minutes (separately), mix and add flour and sugar, a little of each in turn, whisking all the time (the sugar should have been previously warmed and put through a wire sieve, and the flour also warmed). When bubbles begin to appear pour into a tin, scraping out with a knife.

The tin should have been prepared by buttering it, having buttered paper on the bottom,—the whole being powdered with sugar and flour mixed.

Miss HUGHES.

SWISS ROLL.

10 oz. plain flour		2 drops essence of lemon, or,
12 oz. rough castor sugar		if preferred, vanilla
	10 eggs	

Sieve the flour on a piece of clean paper ready for use, break the eggs into a very clean bowl, having no sign of any grease, with the sugar and flavouring; then with your egg-whisk well beat up till quite light and of a nice creamy colour; then mix in your flour lightly. Cover your baking sheet with white paper, then brush the paper well all over with melted lard. Now pour your sponge batter on and level it all over with knife. Bake in a very hot oven for about 5 minutes, or until when you touch it with your finger it leaves no mark upon it. Put some sugar on your board and turn your roll upon it. Strip off the paper, spread jam on it, roll up, dust with sugar.

Mr. THOMAS HILL.

VIENNA BREAD.

Set a ferment with 1 pint of water and 1 pint of milk at 95°, 1 oz. yeast, 1 lb. flour (Vienna), 1 oz. castor sugar. Cover well up, keep in warm place, care being taken not to shake it. When ready add 3 lbs. more flour, 1 oz. salt, and 1 oz. butter, and make up into a very stiff dough,

Thomas Mackay & Sons,

BAKERS, CONFECTIONERS,
AND PURVEYORS,

35 & 37 Main Street, LARGS,

AND

21 West Blackhall St., GREENOCK.

ESTABLISHED 1838.

RESTAURANT — DINNERS, TEAS, LUNCHEONS, Etc., Etc.

SPECIAL TERMS FOR LARGE PARTIES.
PRICES ON APPLICATION.

SPECIALITIES
OF FINEST QUALITY.

MACKAY'S CALF'S FOOT JELLY

Is the perfection of a table Jelly, and is also highly recommended for invalids. In Tumblers at 10d., and in Jars at 1/. Also in Bottles at 1/2, 1/3, and 2/6.

SCOTCH SHORTBREAD.

In Tins at 1/10, 2/4, 3/4, 4/4, and 6/4. In Cakes at 3d., 6d., 1/, 2/, and 3/. WAFER SHORTBREAD AND SHORTBREAD FINGERS in Tins.

OAT CAKES.

Made from the Finest Oatmeal daily. In Packets at 3d. and 6d.

Also Bread, Biscuits, Cakes, &c., in all best varieties.
Fresh Stock always on hand.
Goods for Special Orders are not baked until as near as possible time of delivery

---

Specialities in Wedding Cakes
AND ALL KINDS OF HIGH-CLASS CONFECTIONERY.

Telephone Nos. { 0199 LARGS. 39 X GREENOCK.

giving it plenty of kneading. Cover up for 1 hour, then knead it again and let it stand for another hour. When it is ready make all sorts of fancy loaves,—twists, cres-cents, etc.

Mr. Thomas Hill.

VINEGAR CAKE.

1 lb. flour	1 pint warm milk
1 lb. raisins (stoned)	1 dessert-spoonful of car-
½ lb. butter	bonate of soda mixed
¼lb. mixed peel (cut thin)	with milk
3 oz. moist sugar	1 tablespoonful of vinegar

Mix well. Bake in slow oven for 2 hours.

Mrs. Ellison.

'XMAS CAKE.

¾ lb. butter	½ lb. citron peel
1 lb. sugar	9 eggs
1 lb. flour	½ glassful brandy
2 lbs. currants	Nutmeg, cloves, and cin-
2 lbs. raisins	namon to taste

Beat butter and sugar to a cream, add the eggs well beaten, then the flour, and lastly the fruit and brandy. Steam for 3 hours and bake for 1 hour in a slow oven.

Miss A. H. Carmichael.

SMALL CAKES.

ADELINE CAKES.

½ lb. butter	Blanched almonds
3 oz. castor sugar	3 tablespoonfuls of cream
6 oz. flour	Rind of 1 orange and 1 lemon
3 eggs	3 oz. dried cherries, cut small

Half teaspoonful of baking powder

Beat butter to a cream, add sugar, work eight minutes, add flour and eggs, cream and fruit. Bake about 45 minutes, with almonds on top.

Mrs. Ellison, The Vicarage, Windsor.

ADELAIDE CAKES.

3 oz. Brown & Polson's "Patent" corn flour	3 oz. butter
1 oz. Brown & Polson's Paisley flour	3 oz. sugar
	2 oz. ordinary flour
	3 eggs

Butter a dozen patty tins. Beat butter and sugar to a cream. Beat the eggs well. Mix the three flours well together, add them to the creamed butter and sugar alternately with the eggs, beating well all the time. Bake in the prepared tins for 20 minutes. When ready lay on a wire tray to cool.

MAIRI NIC'LLE MHUNADH,
A'Choille Bheag, Oban.

ARROWROOT DROPS.

2½ lbs. flour	4 eggs
1¼ lbs. butter	½ oz. of carbonate of ammonia
1¼ lbs. sugar	Essence of lemon
4 oz. arrowroot	Milk

Sieve the flour and ammonia on a piece of clean paper with the arrowroot; put the butter and sugar into a bowl and well beat up till quite smooth, then add the flavouring and the eggs, one at a time, well beating between each egg; when light mix in lightly the flour and vol., adding a little milk to make a very soft dough, then get your bag with a plain half-inch tube and half-fill with the mixture, and drop about the size of a walnut on clean buttered sheets. Cool oven, will take about 20 minutes to bake.

Mr. THOMAS HILL.

THE ORIGINAL "BATH BUN."

1¼ lb. flour	Pinch of castor sugar
1 oz. yeast	6 oz. sugar nibs
8 oz. butter	8 oz. sultanas
Spice	6 yolks of eggs
Lemon peel, cut very fine	Milk

Put the flour into a bowl, rub the fine butter into it, dissolve yeast in half-pint warmed milk, add to the flour with the spice, peel, and the pinch (about 1 oz.) of sugar and the egg yolks, then work all together and cover up, and keep in a warm place for two or three hours. Then turn out on your board and add your nibs and sultanas, and chop them into the dough with your knife or scraper ; now, on well-buttered sheets place, roughly, about three ounces each, giving plenty of room. Prove, and when ready wash over with eggs ; wash very lightly, be careful not to knock out the proof, bake in good oven (about 450°) 20 minutes.

Mr. THOMAS HILL.

BREAKFAST ROLLS.

½ lb. flour	Salt
1½ large teaspoonfuls baking powder	Milk

Mix the milk into the other ingredients with a spoon till you have a nice soft dough.   Drop the rolls on to a well buttered tin and bake 10 minutes.   ¼ oz. butter may be added if liked.

BEECHWOOD.

BROWN ROLLS.

1 lb. whole flour	1½ teaspoonfuls baking powder
2 oz. bran, mixed in with the flour	A pinch of salt
	Mix with milk, *not* soft

Bake in a hot oven.

Mrs. W. E. CRUM.

CREAM BISCUITS.

1 lb. of flour	2 tablespoonfuls of cream
2 oz. of butter	A little salt

Roll out *very* thin and prick them.   Cut them as large as a small plate.   They should be short and crisp.   Milk may be used instead of cream.

Mrs. W. E. CRUM.

GINGER BISCUITS. 1.

½ lb. butter	3 oz. preserved ginger, cut into tiny pieces
½ lb. sugar	
½ lb. flour	A little of the ginger juice

Cream butter and sugar together, mix in the flour a little at a time, then put in the ginger and juice.   Press it into small round biscuits shaped with the hand, and bake in not too hot an oven.

Mrs. LE CHALLAS, Glenfinart.

GINGER BISCUITS. 2.

3 oz. butter	4 oz. ginger
2 lbs. flour	Enough new milk to make
4 oz. powdered sugar	a dough

Work into small crumbs, knead into stiff paste with new milk, roll thin and cut out with cutter; bake in slow oven till crisp through and a pale colour.

BEECHWOOD.

SHREWSBURY BISCUITS.

½ lb. flour	¼ lb. butter
¼ lb. sugar	1 beaten egg
½ teaspoonful baking powder	

Beat butter to a cream, add sugar, egg and baking powder, beat all well together, and then add the flour. Roll out ¼ inch thick, cut into round cakes, prick and bake in moderate oven; sprinkle sugar on top of each.

Mrs. SMALL of Dirnanean.

THIN BISCUITS.

2 oz. butter	½ lb. *finest* flour
Enough milk to moisten	

Roll three times, as thin as possible, and prick the biscuits well. Bake in slow oven five or six minutes, then place in front of fire to dry. Always crisp before serving, either before the fire or one minute in oven.

Mrs. PITT-TAYLOR, 85 Queen's Gate, London.

THIN BISCUITS.

2 lbs. of flour	Piece of butter size of a walnut
Salt to taste	Milk and water

Take the flour and salt and rub these together with the butter, moisten with milk and water, and let the paste so produced be as still as possible. Beat with a rolling-pin for 15 minutes, then roll it out very thin and prick it all over. Cut to the size of biscuit wished for, and bake in a quick oven. If the even is slow the biscuits will be tough.

Mrs. W. E. CRUM.

WHITE GINGERBREAD BISCUITS.

½ lb. flour		½ lb. butter
½ lb. sugar		½ oz. ginger
	1 egg	

Rub butter into flour and sugar, then add the ginger, mix it stiff with the egg; roll out and cut in rounds or fingers.

Miss A. PENNIFOLD,
32 Old Queen Street, Westminster.

WINE BISCUITS.

½ lb. of flour		½ pint of cream
½ oz. of butter		Pinch of salt

Mix the ingredients to a stiff dough, roll out to the thickness of half an inch, cut with a 3-inch round cutter, roll out the thickness of a wafer cake; put in a hot oven to crisp.

Mrs. W. E. CRUM.

BRANDY SNAP GINGERBREAD.

10 oz. flour		½ oz. ground ginger
5 oz. butter		¼ oz. mixed spice
7 oz. moist sugar		10 drops essence of
14 oz. syrup		lemon

Melt butter in a large basin; when melted add sugar and syrup and work up well, then add flour and spice and ginger, and mix well, but do not rub too much; this gingerbread dough is better for standing a few days before baking. Well butter your baking sheet, then drop from a bag with plain tube pieces as large as a marble, and allow 3 inches between to allow for flowing. Bake in a very cool oven about 15 minutes; when set take them off the sheet with a thin knife, and whilst soft wrap them round a stick or rolling-pin to curl them; you will have to be quick about it or they will get too brittle to bend.

Mr. THOMAS HILL.

BRANDY SNAPS.

½ oz. ginger		3 oz. sugar
3 oz. butter		3½ oz. flour
6 oz. treacle or syrup		A little cinnamon

Melt butter, sugar, and treacle, add the other ingredients, put little spoonfuls of it (size of a 5/- bit) on a well-buttered baking tin, cook 5 to 10 minutes in brisk oven ; cut into pieces and roll these round a wooden roller (1½ inches in diameter), to cool. They may be filled with whipped cream.

Miss Hughes, Beechwood.

COBURG CAKES.

¼ lb. flour	½ teaspoonful carbonate
¼ lb. butter	of soda
¼ lb. treacle	Almonds
¼ lb. sugar	1 teaspoonful ground ginger
2 eggs	1 teaspoonful cinnamon

Put flour, soda, and spices into a basin and mix; put into a saucepan the treacle, sugar, and butter, and bring to the boil; beat the eggs well, and pour treacle, etc., among them and stir well; pour this mixture into the contents of the basin and beat the whole thoroughly. Butter some small tins and put half an almond in the bottom of each; fill each about three-quarters full, and bake in a moderate oven for 20 minutes.

Miss Black, Oronsay, Connell.

CRUMPETS.

5 lbs. flour	2 quarts milk and water
2 oz. yeast	½ oz salt

Heat milk and water to 95°, dissolve yeast, add to the flour and salt, give it a good stir, then cover up and let stand in a warm place free from draughts for 2 hours.

Mr. Thomas Hill.

LADY DORCHESTER'S CAKES.

(Very old English Recipe.)

1 lb. flour	½ lb. butter
¼ lb. pounded sugar	6 yolks of eggs
A little grated lemon peel	

Rub butter into flour, add sugar, then eggs and then grated lemon peel. Roll them out nearly 1 inch thick, and prick them slightly. Cut them into any shape you please.

Mrs. Small of Dirnanean.

DUTCH CAKES.

2 oz. butter	1 oz. chopped and blanched
2 oz. sugar	almonds
2 oz. flour	1 egg Vanilla essence to taste

Mix butter and sugar thoroughly; add flour, flavour with vanilla, beat and add yolk; roll out to ⅛-inch thickness, cut into shapes, brush with white of egg and sprinkle with almonds. Bake 10 minutes in slow oven.

Miss HUGHES, Beechwood.

GALETTES.

½ lb. flour	1 oz. of castor sugar
3 oz. butter	Pinch of salt
1 egg	Teaspoonful of baking
Gill of milk	powder

Rub the butter lightly into the flour; add the other ingredients, mixing together with the egg and milk. Roll out about ½-inch thick; cut into small cakes with a round cutter. Brush over with beaten egg, and bake in a quick oven for 10 to 15 minutes.

Mrs. JAMES TINNE,
Bashley Lodge, New Forest.

GINGER CAKES.

1 lb. patent flour	½ pint of sour milk
½ lb. plain flour	1 lb. syrup
5 oz. butter	½ oz. ground ginger
6 oz. moist sugar	½ oz. mixed spice

Well rub the butter in the flour, make a "bay," put syrup, sugar, milk, ginger, and spice in; well work up till smooth, then draw in the flours, well mix and give a good working up. Spoon into small rings well buttered, about 3 oz. each. Cool oven, about 1 hour. Be careful not to touch them till quite baked, as they will drop in the centre. Mr. THOMAS HILL.

GINGER NUTS.

½ lb. flour	1 teaspoonful ginger
1 teaspoonful fine oatmeal	1 teaspoonful spice
½ teaspoonful carbonate	3 oz. butter or lard
of soda	1 cupful syrup

Melt the syrup and lard together, and pour into the dry ingredients, work into a dough. Break off pieces the size of a nut and roll into a ball, then flatten slightly, lay on a tin and bake 10 minutes. Miss STORY.

GRIC CAKES.

1 lb. corn flour, mixed with	4 eggs
a little flour	8 oz. sifted sugar
1 oz. fresh butter	2 teaspoonfuls essence of lemon

2 teaspoonfuls baking powder

Beat sugar and butter to a cream, add one egg and a little flour, and so on until these are finished; lastly add baking powder and essence, put into well-buttered patty pans, a teaspoonful in each, and bake in quick oven between seven and ten minutes.

Miss A. H. CARMICHAEL.

GRISSINI, or TURIN BREAD.

12 tablespoonfuls fine flour	3 eggs
2 oz. fresh butter	White of egg

A little salt and a little powdered sugar

Mix all together into a stiff dough, if not stiff enough add flour and sugar. Work it well with the hand, then take off small bits and roll them with the rolling-pin into sticks about 6 or 8 inches long, and as thick as your little finger; glaze with white of egg, and bake in quick oven.

Mrs. SMALL of Dirnanean, Perthshire.

LAWN TENNIS CAKES.

2½ lbs. flour	2 lbs. sultanas
2 lbs. butter	1 lb. mixed peel
2 lbs. castor sugar	1 quart eggs (24)
2 lbs. currants	¼ oz. grated nutmeg

Few drops essence of lemon

Cream up as usual, only be careful to beat well between the eggs, as being very rich it may break or curdle before you get all your eggs in; if it does, take a handful of your flour and add to the batter, and keep on beating. When ready add your plain flour, and mix up lightly; fill into round papered rings, about 18 oz. each, bake in moderate oven one hour. Next day strip off paper, and ice with almond icing (which see), and then ice with water icing, and sprinkle finely-chopped pistachio kernels on top. If small cakes, instead of the pistachios, pipe on a small border with cake icing from a star tube, and trace the outlines of a tennis court upon the top of each.

Mr. THOMAS HILL.

MILK CAKES.

Take 1 lb. of flour, a little salt, mix with as much thick cream as will make it into a soft paste. Roll out very thin, cut into rounds the size of a small plate, prick with a biscuit pricker, and bake in a quick oven.

Mrs. SANDBACH.

Milk Cakes Baked on Hot Plate.

2 quarts milk and water	1 oz. salt
3 oz. yeast	Flour
Handful of sugar	

Dissolve yeast in a little warm water, then heat the two quarts of milk and water to 100° and add the flour very lightly, making a very thin batter. When ready add salt and a handful of sugar and more flour. The batter must be very thin; let it stand half-an-hour, then give it a good stir up, and ladle it out on to your hot plate to bake. Turn each one over when half-done.

Mr. THOMAS HILL.

HOT MUFFINS.

2 oz. Brown & Polson's Paisley flour	1 teaspoonful of sugar
1 lb. ordinary flour	1 egg
1 oz. butter	1 teaspoonful of salt
	½ pint of sweet milk

Sift the flours, sugar and salt together into a basin. Rub the butter into the flour with the tips of the fingers. Make into a moderately soft dough with the beaten egg and milk. Roll out flat on a floured board till about half-an-inch thick. Cut into rounds with floured cutter, dipping your cutter frequently into the flour to prevent the dough sticking to it. Place the muffins on an oven-shelf, and bake for seven minutes.

MAIRI NIC'LLE MHUNADH.

MUFFINS.

9 lbs. flour	2 quarts water
4 oz. yeast	1 pint milk
½ oz. salt	

Heat liquor to 100°, ferment with 3 lbs. of flour; when ready add the 6 lbs. flour and salt; make a nice soft dough ; prove well, when proved weigh 3 oz. pieces, roll up into round balls, flatten out a very little, and place on boards well dusted with rice flour, then put in your prover with a little steam. When proved enough take off boards with a palette knife, and bake on your hot plate slightly greased. When done, brush off all flour.

Mr. THOMAS HILL.

OAT CAKES.

2 large breakfastcupfuls of fine oatmeal		Pinch salt
Pinch carbonate of soda		1 tablespoonful of fresh lard or beef dripping
	1 teacupful hot water	

Put meal in large bowl, adding the soda and salt. Rub into the meal the dripping or lard, mix with the water. Roll out on baking board, having your board well dusted with meal. Cut in squares and bake on hot girdle. When hardened on girdle toast in front of clear fire.

Miss A. H. CARMICHAEL.

PARKINS.

3 lbs. patent flour		1½ lbs. raw sugar
2 lbs. medium oatmeal		3 lbs. syrup
1 lb. lard		1 oz. spice
	1 oz. ground ginger	

Mix flour and oatmeal ; make a " bay," put lard, sugar and spices, and syrup in, and give it a good rubbing until you have a nice smooth paste, then draw in the flour and make into a soft dough, spoon into small rings or hoops, well buttered, about 3 ozs. each. Very slow oven. Will take 30 to 40 minutes. Mr. THOMAS HILL.

PARKINS.

1 lb. flour		1 oz. carbonate of soda
1 lb. fine oatmeal		
5 oz. lard		Essence of almonds
1 lb. syrup		8 oz. raw sugar

Mix into a nice dough, with a little milk if required. Weigh off 3 oz. each, roll up into round balls, set 3 inches apart on a well-buttered sheet, wash with egg, put a half almond (blanched) on top of each, and bake in a very cool oven about half an hour. Mr. THOMAS HILL.

QUEEN DROPS (Rich).

10 oz. flour	1 oz. lemon peel, cut in
8 oz. sugar	very small cubes
8 oz. butter	5 eggs
4 oz. currants	A little milk

Same as for Arrowroot Drops.

Mr. THOMAS HILL.

QUEEN CAKES (Rich).

6 oz. plain flour	4 oz. currants
4 oz. butter	Enough carbonate of am-
4 oz. castor sugar	monia (vol.) to cover a
3 eggs	sixpence

No milk

Sieve flour and vol. together, put sugar and butter in a large basin, with 3 drops of essence of lemon, and beat up well with a wooden spatula or large spoon; then add the eggs, one at a time, beating well between each egg. When well up, fill into heart-shaped tins with a palette knife. Good hot oven, about 15 minutes.

Mr. THOMAS HILL.

RICE DROPS.

2 lbs. patent flour	3 eggs
1 lb. castor sugar	½ pint sweet milk
5 oz. butter	Rice flour

Weigh flour on the board, make a bay, then put butter, sugar and eggs in the centre, rub together to a smooth mass so that you cannot feel the grain of the sugar, then add the milk and draw in the flour, making a nice soft dough; weigh 3 oz. each, roll up into balls, wash with milk, and dip each one in rice flour, and place on a clean well-buttered baking sheet, about 2 inches apart, with a small piece of lemon peel on top.

Bake in a cool oven (400°), a pale colour, about 20 minutes.

Mr. THOMAS HILL.

RICE CAKES.

4 eggs	Weight of 3 eggs in sugar
Weight of 2 eggs in flour	½ oz. baking powder
Weight of 1 egg in rice	3 oz. warmed butter

Beat eggs and sugar together, add flour and rice and butter, beat for 5 minutes, and bake in moderate oven for 10 minutes to a quarter of an hour.

BEECHWOOD.

ROCK BUNS.

½ lb. flour		1 egg
2 oz. butter		¼ lb. currants
1 dessert-spoonful baking		3 tablespoonfuls sugar
powder		Milk
	Salt	

Wet all (except salt) with a little warm milk. Mix the rest of the milk and egg together, add salt and bake in a moderate oven.

Mrs. CAMPBELL of Inverneill.

BREAKFAST SCONES.

2 cupfuls of flour		Piece of butter the size of a
2 teaspoonfuls baking powder		walnut
	Milk	

Mix with milk *very* lightly. Rub over with beaten egg and bake very quickly. The goodness of the scones depends entirely on the mixing, which must be done very lightly or they will be heavy.

ALLERTON.

BUTTER SCONES.

1 lb. flour		½ small teaspoonful car-
¼ lb. butter		bonate of soda
	Milk	

Rub the butter into the flour and carbonate of soda, with enough cold milk to form a soft paste. Roll out to about a quarter of an inch thick, cut into rounds about 3 inches across, and fry in butter till a nice light brown. To be eaten hot with jam.

Mrs. MACDONALD of Dunach.

DROP SCONES. 1.

6 tablespoonfuls flour		½ teaspoonful cream of
1 tablespoonful sugar		tartar
½ teaspoonful carbonate of		2 eggs in 4 teacupfuls
soda		of milk

Whip the eggs and milk together; add the other in-gredients; grease the girdle, and drop on about a table-spoonful. Turn with a knife.

Miss S. PILKINGTON, Sandside.

DROP SCONES. 2.

6 cupfuls flour	1 teaspoonful cream of tartar
2 teaspoonfuls soda	3 tablespoonfuls sugar
Buttermilk	

Mix all into a stiff batter and drop them on to a greased girdle. Flour and eat.

Miss HUGHES.

FLOUR CAKES.

1 lb. flour	The white of 1 egg
2 oz. butter	A spoonful of yeast
Milk	

Take the flour and rub in the butter, add to it the white of the egg well beaten, work up the yeast and mix with the egg; then make it into paste with a little warm milk. Let it stand to rise, and roll the cakes out an hour before you send them to the oven.

Miss L. M'INROY of Lude.

GIRDLE CAKES. 1.

Equal quantities of flour and butter, a little salt. Mix with milk (if with cream half the butter will do), roll out ¼ inch thick, cut in small rounds about 3 inches across and bake on a girdle over the fire (a frying-pan will do). The cakes are to be baked on both sides, then split and buttered and served very hot. They require to be made fresh, as they will not warm up.

Mrs. CAMPBELL of Inverneill.

GIRDLE CAKES. 2.

4 lbs. patent flour	6 oz. sugar
6 oz. lard	½ oz. salt

Rub the lard, sugar and salt into the flour, mix up with buttermilk into a nice soft dough; let it stand half-an-hour, then weigh 4 oz. each, flatten with your pin and put on your hot plate; when half done, turn.

Mr. THOMAS HILL.

GIRDLE SCONES. 1.

2½ breakfast-cupfuls of flour	Pinch of salt
1 teaspoonful cream of tartar	1 oz. butter
1 teaspoonful carbonate of soda	1 teaspoonful golden syrup

Buttermilk

Put the flour, cream of tartar, soda, and salt through a
hair sieve into a basin, mix the butter into the flour
through the fingers. Pour the buttermilk in, stirring with
a knife till it is of a soft consistency. Turn out and roll
quickly. Cut into shapes and bake on a very hot girdle
for 10 minutes.

Mrs. W. E. CRUM.

GIRDLE SCONES. 2.

3 breakfast-cupfuls flour	1 teaspoonful fine salt
1 teaspoonful cream of tartar	1 dessert-spoonful syrup
1 teaspoonful carbonate of soda	Buttermilk

Sift the flour into a large bowl, lightly mix with it the
carbonate of soda, cream of tartar, and salt, put in the
syrup, and then moisten with fresh buttermilk; mix well,
roll out on baking board and cut into squares, and bake
on hot girdle.

Miss A. H. CARMICHAEL,

Altavona House, Oban.

PETTICOAT TAILS.

(Old Scotch Recipe.)

6 oz. butter	1 lb. flour
6 oz. sugar	A little water

Fine sugar

Rub butter and sugar into the flour, add water and work
to a smooth dough. Divide into two, roll into two round
cakes about the size of a large dinner plate. Cut a round
cake from the centre of each with a cutter 4 inches in
diameter, then cut the outside of each into 8 pieces, prick
the tops, dust over with fine sugar, and bake in a moderate
oven for half-an-hour. Lay one round on a plate and lay
the 8 petticoats round it.

Mrs. SMALL of Dirnanean.

POTATO SCONES. 1.

2 lbs. flour	1 oz. butter
½ teaspoonful baking soda	Pinch of salt
6 potatoes	Buttermilk

Put the flour in a basin, adding the potatoes (mashed), the soda, butter and salt, and mix well with buttermilk; then roll out thin, place on a very hot girdle, and turn when brown.

Mrs. JOHN STEWART, Fairlie.

POTATO SCONES. 2.

½ lb. flour	3 oz. butter
6 oz. mashed potatoes	A little water

Rub the butter and flour together, then add the potatoes; mix with a little water; roll the paste out about an inch thick, or thinner as preferred. Cut into rounds, and bake in a quick oven.

Mrs. F. BATESON,
Bell Farm, Clewer, Windsor.

POTATO CAKES.

1 pint mashed potatoes	½ teaspoonful salt
1 teaspoonful baking powder	1 tablespoonful butter
2 tablespoonfuls flour	

Roll out to quarter of an inch in thickness, and bake in hot oven. Split and butter well.

Mrs. CAMPBELL of Inverneill.

RICE SCONES.

Boil rice with milk till it is well cooked, but not too soft. When ready remove the pan from the fire till cooled a *little*. Then stir flour into it till it is a proper consistency for scones. Handle as little as possible. Roll out and cut, and bake on girdle.

Mrs. W. E. CRUM.

Historic Cookbooks of the World

SCONES.

Put a pint of milk on the fire, and while it is boiling sprinkle in flour till it is thick as porridge, add a little salt. Take it out of the pan, and roll it like paste into thin cakes. Put them on the frying-pan, and bake till they brown a little.

BEECHWOOD.

SCONES.

1 lb flour	3 teaspoonfuls baking powder
1 oz. butter	A little salt Milk

Rub butter and baking powder into flour and salt. Mix into a light dough with milk. Roll out and cut, and bake in a hot oven.

Mrs. G. FLETCHER, Plumridge Farm,
Stag Hill, Barnet.

"HIGHLAND SHORTBREAD." 1.

1 lb. flour	½ lb. fresh butter
4 oz. sifted sugar	

Work the flour and sugar into the butter, then halve the dough and knead it out into two rounds, nick round edges with thumb and prick with fork, divide the rounds in four, and bake in a moderate oven.

Miss M. BLACK, Oronsay, Connell.

SHORTBREAD. 2.

1½ lbs. flour	6 or 8 oz. sugar
1 lb. butter (half fresh half salt)	4 oz. rice flour

Beat the butter to a cream, work all together into a dough, make it into round cakes, ornament with orange peel, bake on tins in a moderate oven.

Mrs. MACAULAY, The Manse, Reay.

SPONGE CAKES.

4 oz. flour | 4 oz. sugar
2 eggs

Beat the sugar and eggs well together, add the flour, beating all the time. Butter small patty pans, sprinkle bottom of each with sugar and half-fill with mixture. Bake in quick oven for 15 or 20 minutes.

Miss M. BLACK, Oronsay, Connell.

HALF-DOZEN TEACAKES.

2 oz. butter | 1 egg
1 lb. flour | 1 gill milk
2d. worth of German barm

Rub butter into flour, make a hole in the middle to receive beaten-up egg, barm and milk, cover it over with the flour, &c., as you would do bread dough, and leave it to rise; work it up again and leave it to rise a little longer. Divide into six, and bake 20 minutes.

Miss ELLEN WILLIAMS.

TEACAKES.

(Called Fat Rascals in Yorkshire.)

Work a good proportion of butter into some flour, mix to a proper consistency with thin cream; roll out thin, and cut out with a round cutter. Bake half-an-hour. Split and butter them while very hot.

Mrs. SMALL of Dirnanean.

TROCADERO CAKES.

2 lbs. patent flour	½ lb sultanas
1 lb. butter	1 lb. lemon peel
1 lb. castor sugar	4 oz. ginger chips
1½ lbs. eggs (weighed in the shells)	Milk
	Essence of lemon

Weigh flour on your board, put butter and sugar in a bowl, warm a little, then well cream up, adding the eggs two at a time, beating up well between each ; when nice and light add flour, fruit, peel and ginger chips, use a little milk to get it to a nice batter consistency; now, having your hoops or rings papered inside, weigh your batter (18 ozs.) into each ring ; place in a medium oven (400°) about 45 minutes, or try by putting a wire into the cake, then drawing it out and drawing the wire between your finger and thumb ; if it is sticky it is not done, if quite dry then the cake is done. Let it stand till next day, then take off the paper, and ice all over with fondant or royal icing, coloured green, and when nearly set hard roll the cake in finely-chopped pistachio kernels.

Mr. Thomas Hill.

VICTORIA BUNS.

4 lb. flour	1 oz. cream of tartar
1½ lbs. butter	½ oz. carbonate of soda
1½ lbs. castor sugar	6 eggs
8 oz. sultanas	A little nutmeg
4 oz. orange peel, cut fine	Milk
A few drops of orange flavouring	

Rub butter in flour, weigh your flour on the board, make a bay, put in your sugar, sultanas and peel ; beat up your eggs and add them, draw in your flour, add a little milk if necessary to make soft dough ; weigh 4 oz. each, place on well-buttered sheets 2 inches apart, wash with milk and dust with sugar. Place in a hot oven (450°) ; mind that the bottoms do not burn, as they take fire very soon.

Mr. Thomas Hill.

ADDITIONAL RECIPES.

ADDITIONAL RECIPES.

ADDITIONAL RECIPES.

Story & Triggs.

MODERN AND ANTIQUE HOUSE FURNISHINGS. ::

The "CHEYNE"
Mahogany **Chair**, loose seat,
covered in tapestry,
28/9

The "CHEYNE"
Mahogany **Arm Chair**, loose seat,
covered in tapestry,
39/9

"WALMER."

Mahogany Sheraton
Sideboard inlaid
with kingwood. Ser-
pentine shaped front.
4 feet 6 inches wide,
3 feet high, 22 inches
deep.

£8 15 0

CARRIAGE PAID ON ORDERS 20/- UPWARDS.
— ILLUSTRATED CATALOGUE POST FREE. —

152 to 156
QUEEN VICTORIA STREET, **London, E.C.**

BEVERAGES.

ATHOLE BROSE.

1 lb. dripped honey	1½ pints whisky
About a cupful of cold water	

Put the honey in a basin and add sufficient cold water to dissolve it; stir with a *silver* spoon, and when honey and water are well mixed, add by degrees the whisky, and stir briskly till a froth begins to rise. Bottle and keep tightly corked. [The above proportions have sometimes to be altered slightly, as so much depends on the strength of the whisky and thickness of the honey.]

Miss L. M'INROY of Lude.

CHERRY BRANDY.

Select ripe wild cherries when perfectly black. Fill a large prune bottle three-quarters full with the cherries, then fill up the bottle with candy sugar, and pour in as much brandy as the bottle will hold. When the sugar is melted it is fit for use.

Mrs. MACDONALD of Dunach.

HIGHLAND BITTERS (very old).

1¾ oz. gentian root	½ oz. camomile flower
½ oz. bitter orange peel	½ oz. cinnamon stick
1 oz. coriander seed	½ oz. cloves (whole)

All to be bruised; root cut in small pieces, and peel ditto. Sufficient for two bottles of whisky. Let it soak for about 10 days, then strain off and put more whisky on. It does for a good long time without adding more stuff.

Mrs. MACDONALD of Dunach.

RECIPES FOR CUPS

From the University of Oxford.

I.—CHAMPAGNE CUP.—To one bottle of champagne add
1½ wineglassfuls sherry or marsala, ½ wineglassful brandy,
1 liqueur-glassful curaçoa, 2 bottles soda water, rind of 1
lemon cut thin, with 3 or 4 drops of juice of the lemon.
(Should the champagne be very dry, a teaspoonful of
sugar-syrup should be used.)

2.—MOSELLE CUP.—Same as Champagne Cup, only
more sweetened.

3.—CIDER CUP.—Same as Champagne, except using
lemonade instead of soda water, and the quantity per
quart of cider.

4.—CLARET CUP.—To one bottle claret add 1½ wineglassfuls of good port, 1 liqueur-glassful curaçoa, 1 bottle
lemonade, and 1 bottle soda water, the rind of 1 lemon
cut thin and 3 or 4 drops juice. If they can be got, a few
sprigs of borage will greatly improve this cup.

5.—MULLED CLARET.—Get ¼ lb. cinnamon and ¼ lb.
cloves, put them into a saucepan with 3 pints of water,
and simmer for 1 hour. Strain it off and put 1 wineglassful to every bottle of claret, 1 wineglassful of port ;
add sugar to taste, and serve up with 3 or 4 slices of
lemon in it.

TO MAKE GOOD COFFEE.

½ lb. coffee		1 pint water
	1 egg	

Smash up an egg and its shell into the dry coffee and stir
them round in the pot ; have ready the boiling water and
pour it on the coffee ; leave it to boil up ; pour it back-
wards and forwards from one pot to another once or twice,
and add a *little* cold water to clear it. The shell will
sink to the bottom with the grounds.

OLD RECIPE.

Another Recipe.

Take equal parts of Mocha, Java, and Plantation coffee, ground fine (two good spoonfuls for each person). Place these in an ordinary percolator (after the pot has been thoroughly heated with water), ram the coffee down very hard with the stamper, replace the pierced piece and drop on *boiling* water very slowly, standing the pot on a hob or stove while the water runs through. Use very little water, so as to make an essence of coffee, and fill up each cup with three-quarters or more of milk.

Miss C. PHILLOTTS,
6 Downshire Hill, Hampstead, London.

OLD FASHIONED GINGER BEER.

10 gallons water	8 oz. ginger
10 lbs. lump sugar	5 whites of eggs
8 oz. cream of tartar	10 lemons

½ pint brewers' barm

Crush the ginger, put into a large tub with cream of tartar and the lemons sliced up, boil 2 gallons of the water and pour over the articles in the cover over, and let stand for three hours, then add the sugar and the other eight gallons of water (5 gallons boiling and 3 gallons cold), stir, when cool enough to set to work (80° to 85°) add half pint of brewers' barm, well beat up the whites of eggs and stir well in with the barm, let it work well.

This ginger beer must not be used for sale without a licence, it containing a large amount of spirits.

Mr. THOMAS HILL,
12 Gladstone Road, Seacombe.

GINGER BEER.

2 gallons boiling water	2 lemons sliced
2 oz. cream of tartar	2 lbs. sugar, nearly pennyworth
2½ oz. well bruised ginger root	German barm (or less brewers' barm)

Pour the water over all (except the barm) in a large pan. When half warm take a *little* in a basin and put the barm in it, and when it is well risen pour very gently into the pan to the rest. Let it stand all night, strain through muslin, bottle and well cork it.

Miss ELLEN DUNSBEE, Fulwood.

GINGER WINE.

28 gallons water	38 lemons
94 lbs. fine sugar	3 lbs. refined sugar
3 lbs. unbleached ginger	5 bottles of brandy
3 oz. isinglass	Toast
13 lbs. raisins	Barm

Add the 94 lbs. sugar and the ginger to the water (the ginger should be put in a bag), boil until the scum has done rising, which is usually about half-an-hour, skim it very well. Have ready the raisins in a tub with the lemon rinds pared very thin, pour the boiling liquid on them and let it cool. When it is lukewarm put into it some toast spread with barm. Let it remain 24 hours, then put it in the cask. Squeeze the juice of the lemons on the 3 lbs. of refined sugar, put it in the cask, add the isinglass (dissolved) and the brandy. Stop the cask loosely until it has done working over, when it must be stopped up tight.

Mrs. RENDEL.

VERY GOOD LEMONADE.

3 lemons	6 oz. loaf sugar
6 pints of boiling water	2 glasses of sherry
White of 1 egg	

Pare the lemons very thinly and squeeze out all the juice. Put juice, peel and sugar in a large basin, and pour over them the boiling water, let it all get cold. Have ready a glass jug with the sherry and stiffly-whipped white of egg in it. Pour the strained lemonade into it over these. Add ice if required.

Mrs. LE CHALLAS, Glenfinart. Ardentinny.

LEMON SYRUP.

6 lbs. loaf sugar	¼ lb. concentrated soluble
7¼ ozs. citric acid (in crystals)	essence of lemon
	3¼ pints boiling water

Dissolve the sugar in 2½ pints of boiling water, and the citric acid in ¾ pint of boiling water. When quite dissolved put the two together. Leave standing till quite cold, then add the lemon essence and stir up well, and bottle it, putting it through a fine strainer. About a tablespoonful to a tumbler of water.

"OLD MAN'S MILK."

1 quart whipped cream	½ bottle sherry
1 bottle claret	½ bottle port
½ bottle brandy	½ lb. white sugar, crushed

Put the claret in a large silver bowl, let some slices of lemon float in it for two hours, then add the other ingredients (omitting the cream). Then take out the lemon and add the cream. Set it on ice for three hours, and serve.

Miss E. McIntyre.

ORANGE BRANDY.

1 dozen Seville oranges	1 gallon best pale French
4 lbs. bruised sugar candy	brandy

Put the oranges and brandy in an earthen jar and cover it so that it is air-tight. Turn the top layer of oranges every three or four days; when they have become quite hard, which they will be in a month, the brandy will be fit to bottle. Add the sugar when the oranges are taken out. Bottle the brandy in pints. The oranges may be pricked with a fork before being put into the brandy.

Another Recipe.

Peel of 8 Seville oranges	1 gallon new strong pale
and 8 lemons	brandy
3 lbs. fine loaf sugar or sugar candy	

Cut the peel very thin into the brandy in a jar with a cover, add the sugar, and stir the whole well twice a day for three days. Strain and bottle in white glass bottles, and let it stand on end till clear and the sediment quite settled. Draw off as much as will run quite clear; strain the remainder, let it stand till again clear.

Mrs. W. E. Crum.

PINEAPPLE SYRUP,

Remove the core and rind, weigh the remaining fruit, take an equal weight of moist sugar. Mince the fruit finely, put in one layer half of the sugar on a dish and spread the fruit in it, covering it with the other half of the sugar. Let this remain between two dishes for 24 hours or longer. Place the whole in a copper or enamelled pan and boil for not less than one hour, stirring frequently. As some pines give out more juice than others, it is sometimes necessary to boil several hours to reduce to a thick liquid, which, when cold, should be of the consistency of condensed milk. For diphtheria use one teaspoonful to every gill of boiling water, to which add the juice of $\frac{1}{2}$ a lime.—Copyright, by permission of the West Indian Produce Association, Ltd., 4 Fenchurch Buildings, London, E.C.

A PLEASANT DRINK.

| $\frac{1}{2}$ oz. cream of tartar | Peel of one orange |
| $\frac{1}{4}$ lb. white sugar | 3 thin slices of lemon |

3 pints boiling water

To stand for 2 hours before using.

BEECHWOOD.

ROWANBERRY LIQUEUR.

| 1 pint brandy | 1 pint syrup |

1 handful picked rowan berries

The berries must be dried till shrivelled, then placed in brandy and left from a week to 10 days. Then strain, and mix with an equal quantity of thick, very clear syrup made with loaf sugar in a brass boiler.

Mrs. W. E. CRUM.

SLOE WHISKY.

| 10 lbs. sloes | $7\frac{1}{2}$ lbs. sugar (white) |

$2\frac{1}{2}$ gallons best whisky

Put into 5-gallon jar, well corked, and shake daily for a month. Then strain off and bottle.

Mrs. MACDONALD of Dunach.

RASPBERRY ACID.

| 12 lbs. raspberries. | 5 oz. tartaric acid |
| 2 quarts spring water, boiled and gone cold. | 1¼ lbs. loaf sugar to every pint of juice. |

Dissolve the tartaric acid in the water, pour on the raspberries, let it stand 24 hours. To each pint of juice add 1½ lbs. sugar, stir until the sugar is quite dissolved, and then put in small bottles. It is useful as a beverage mixed with water, and also for flavouring creams and jellies.

Mrs. CAMPBELL of Inverneill.

RASPBERRY VINEGAR.

| 1 lb. raspberries | White wine vinegar |
| 1 lb. lump sugar | |

Put the raspberries into a china bowl with as much of the vinegar as will cover them. (It must be a china bowl, as the acid corrodes the glazing of common earthen vessels, and makes any mixture poisonous.) Let it stand 24 hours, then strain it through a cloth to get the juice out of the raspberries, put in the sugar and boil it till clarified; then bottle it for use. It is a pleasant drink mixed with water.

Miss L. M'INROY of Lude.

RASPBERRY VINEGAR.

| 2 quarts raspberries | 1 quart best white wine |
| Loaf sugar | vinegar |

Put a quart of raspberries in a bowl, and pour upon it a quart of the best white wine vinegar. The next day, strain the liquor over a quart of fresh raspberries, to stand the same time. The raspberries may be slightly bruised. Then drain the liquor from them without pressing, and run through a flannel bag previously wetted with vinegar to prevent waste. Put it into a stone jar (not glazed), with 1 lb. of loaf sugar to every pint of juice. Put the jar into a saucepan of water. Let it simmer about an hour and skim it; or you may boil it in a brass kettle, which is less trouble. When cold, bottle it, but do not let it remain in the kettle after it is done.

Mrs. W. E. CRUM.

ADDITIONAL RECIPES.

ADDITIONAL RECIPES.

Folklore and Mythology Archive

SAUCES, Etc.

BERKSHIRE PICKLE (for Hams or Bacon).

½ oz. saltpetre	1 oz. black pepper
¼ lb. bay salt	½ oz. ground allspice
¼ lb. common salt	½ lb. coarse sugar

1 quart strong ale

Boil all together, and pour immediately on the hams.
Turn every day in the pickle for three weeks.

BIGNON'S SAUCE FOR COLD LAMB.

Take the same quantity of capers, parsley, chives, gherkins, and tarragon. Mince the whole of them very fine,
mix together, season with pepper, salt, and cayenne, and
put it into a jar with tarragon vinegar. When required,
put a sufficient quantity into a bowl with plenty of finely-
minced chervil and a little French mustard and salad oil
to taste.

Miss CAMPBELL of Jura.

BRANDY BUTTER. 1.

Take ½ lb. of butter and work into a cream (do not heat
the butter), then work into the mixture very gradually ½
pint brandy; lastly add sugar to taste very lightly, and
set to get cold. The secret of this recipe is that the sugar
must not be added until the brandy has thoroughly mixed
with the butter.

Mrs. EVELYN PARKER,
Ravenscroft, Aigburth, Liverpool.

BRANDY BUTTER. 2.

2 oz. fresh butter	Whites of 2 eggs
4 oz. castor sugar	1 tablespoonful brandy
A grate of nutmeg (optional)	

Cream the butter, gradually work in the sugar, beating it all till it is light, then mix in (one at a time) the whites of egg, whisking again till it is all light and frothy, and beating in the brandy. Put on ice to harden. If liked, a grate of nutmeg may be strewn over it.

Mrs. W. E. CRUM.

BRAWN SAUCE.

Mix 1 tablespoonful mustard with $\frac{1}{2}$ tablespoonful moist sugar, 2 tablespoonfuls salad oil, and 4 tablespoonfuls vinegar.

BEECHWOOD.

BREAD SAUCE.

Bread	Onion
Milk	Peppercorns
Fresh butter	

It is very important that the bread should be grated from a tin loaf, and allowed to dry in a paper bag some time before using it. It is quite impossible to make good bread sauce with new bread. Cut up an onion in rather large pieces, boil it in milk and pass it through a sieve, or remove the onion. Pour the milk boiling over the crumbs, and add a few peppercorns. Boil the whole in a china saucepan for about 20 minutes. As the milk is absorbed, add a little more until it is an even mass, neither too moist nor too dry. Remove the peppercorns before serving, and stir in a piece of fresh butter. Many people add cream, which spoils it.

Mrs. CHAS. BRUCE.

CHUTNEY.

8 oz. sharp apples, pared, cored and cut in small squares	4 oz. stoned raisins
8 oz. green tomatoes, skinned and cut into pieces	4 oz. sultanas
8 oz. salt	2 oz. cayenne
8 oz. brown sugar	4 oz. powdered ginger
	4 oz. onions, chopped small
	2 quarts vinegar

Mix all well together, and put in a large and well-covered jar. Keep in a wa   place and stir every day for a month. Strain, but   not squeeze. Store the chutney in jars, and bottle the liquor, as it makes an excellent sauce.

CHUTNEY SAUCE.

1 lb. brown sugar	½ lb. ground ginger
1 lb. sultanas	2 oz. salt
1 oz. garlic	Saltspoonful of cayenne
½ lb. onions	3 pints best vinegar

18 good-sized apples

Peel and core the apples, then boil them to a pulp in the vinegar. The other ingredients to be pounded in a mortar, then added to the pulp when cold, and well mixed. It is then ready to bottle.

Mrs. W. E. CRUM.

CUCUMBER VINEGAR.

15 good-sized cucumbers	A small piece of garlic
3 pints vinegar	2 large spoonfuls salt
4 large onions	3 teaspoonfuls pepper
2 shallots	½ teaspoonful cayenne

Slice the cucumbers and onions and put with the other ingredients into a stone jar. Leave it to stand four days, then boil; leave it to get cold, then strain, filter the liquor through fine muslin or flannel and cork up.

Mrs SANDBACH.

CUMBERLAND SAUCE.

Rind and juice of 2 Seville oranges	½ pint port wine
1 lb. red currant jelly	½ teaspoonful cinnamon powder

Cut the orange rind into Italienne shreds (free from white pith), parboil and drain on a sieve; put the orange juice,

currant jelly, port wine and cinnamon in a stewpan,
simmer the whole together and use when cold. A piece
of cinnamon stick may be used instead of the powder. If
it is tied down it will keep some time.

Mrs. CHAS. BRUCE.

CURRY POWDER.

A good West Indian curry powder can be made of 1 oz.
of cayenne, 2 oz. of mustard, 2 oz. of ginger, 4 oz. of fenu-
greek, 4 oz. of cinnamon, 8 oz. of coriander seed, and 3 oz.
of turmeric, or more or less in proportion, well mixed.—
Copyright, by kind permission of the West Indian Produce
Association, Ltd., 4 Fenchurch Buildings, London, E.C.

DUTCH SAUCE. 1.

1 tablespoonful of fine flour.	2 oz. of butter
2 tablespoonfuls of cold water.	Juice of half a lemon or tea-
½ of a pint of boiling water	spoonful of vinegar.
Pinch of salt	Yolks of 2 eggs

Mix a tablespoonful of fine flour in two of cold water, stir it
into a quarter of a pint of fast boiling water, stir it over the fire
until properly thickened, then add a pinch of salt, 2 oz. of
butter broken up, and, when well mixed, the juice of half a
lemon or a teaspoonful of vinegar. Lastly, put in carefully the
yolks of 2 eggs lightly beaten, and, having stirred over a slow
fire for 5 minutes, serve in a tureen. The sauce should be as
thick as very good cream.

Mrs. W. E. CRUM, Fyfield.

DUTCH SAUCE. 2.

1 teaspoonful flour	½ lb. fresh butter
4 tablespoonfuls vinegar (or	Yolks of 5 eggs
Tarragon vinegar)	A little salt and cayenne

Put all in a stewpan (except cayenne and some of the salt),
keep continually stirring. When it has acquired thickness enough, stir it well that you may refine it. Season
with salt and cayenne; strain, if necessary.

Mrs. CAMPBELL of Inverneill.

GOOSEBERRY CHUTNEY.

2 quarts green gooseberries	1 lb. brown sugar
1 lb. raisins, stoned and chopped fine	½ oz. cayenne
	¼ oz. salt

3 pints vinegar

Boil the gooseberries, sugar and raisins as for jam ; then add the other ingredients and boil again 20 minutes.

HOT VINEGAR.

About 1 quart good brown vinegar	1 head of garlic
1 oz. cayenne	1 tablespoonful soy
	2 tablespoonfuls walnut ketchup

Put half the vinegar in a quart wine bottle, add the other ingredients, let it stand 3 or 4 days, shaking it well each day, then fill up with the rest of the vinegar, and cork close.

Mrs. CAMPBELL of Inverneill.

LIVER KETCHUP.

A cow's liver (as dark as possible)	2 oz. whole black pepper
3 salt herrings	2 oz. whole Jamaica pepper
A large bunch of celery	1 oz. cloves
The whites of 3 eggs	½ lb. salt

A little cayenne

Take the liver, cut it down into pieces about an inch square, and with the herrings (cut down) and the celery, put into a large pot with a choppie more water than covers it ; after it boils let it simmer 16 hours, taking great care that it never goes off the boil. Next strain it and cast the whites of the eggs very well, put them (with the shells of the eggs) into the ketchup, put it on the fire, and let it boil for five minutes, take it off and strain it through a jelly bag ; then take the peppers, cloves, salt, and cayenne, mix all with the juice, put it on the fire and boil it 20 minutes. Bottle it with the peppers, and let it stand 24 hours before corking it ; let it be well sealed. If not dark enough, burn a small quantity refined sugar, and mix it with the ketchup the last time before taking it off the fire.

Miss L. M'INROY of Lude.

COLD MÂITRE D'HÔTEL SAUCE. 1.

| 4 oz. fresh butter | 2 teaspoonfuls Tarragon vinegar |
| 1 tablespoonful chopped parsley | or lemon juice |

A little pepper and salt

Knead all together on a plate.

Mrs. SANDBACH.

MÂITRE D'HÔTEL (Cold). 2.

| A piece of fresh butter | Some parsley minced |
| Salt | Pepper |

The juice of 1 lemon, or 2 or 3 drops of vinegar.

Place a hollow plate with all the ingredients on the top of a pan of boiling water for 1 moment, in order to soften the butter without allowing it to melt. Serve this sauce with meat or grilled fish.

Mrs. CAMERON, National Bank House,
Lochmaben.

MAYONNAISE SAUCE.

| Yolks of 2 fresh eggs | A few drops Tarragon |
| 1 gill salad oil | (or Chilli) vinegar |

Pepper and salt

Work the yolks, pepper and salt quickly about in a basin with a wooden spoon, being careful always to stir the same way, add the salad oil by degrees, and drop in the vinegar.

Miss HUGHES.

ITALIAN MINT SAUCE.

Spinach and fresh mint pounded in a mortar and passed through a sieve ; add a little vinegar and very little sugar. The purée ought to be a little thicker than cream and very smooth.

Mrs. SMALL of Dirnanean.

NUT SAUCE (for Poultry and Game).

A coffeecupful of nuts (almonds, cashews, chestnuts, pignole walnuts, &c., as you please)
1 oz. or so of butter
Salt
Pepper

About 1 gill clear stock
½ oz. roux (or ¼ oz. each flour and butter mixed over the fire till smooth)
Yolk of 1 egg.
1 or 2 spoonfuls milk or cream

Scald, blanch, dry and chop the nuts fairly fine, then fry to a pale golden fawn in the butter, and season. Then pound them smooth, add them and the stock to the roux, gradually and alternately, till the materials are all used and the mixture is of a nice consistency ; add the yolk at the last, beaten up in the milk or cream, to the boiling purée. Devilled and salted almonds make a nice but strongly flavoured brown nut sauce, but for this let the nuts colour rather more highly.

Mrs. W. E. CRUM.

ORINOCO SAUCE
(for Plum or Brown Pudding).

¼ lb. butter
Just over ¼ lb. finely powdered sugar

1 tablespoonful brandy
2 tablespoonfuls white wine
A *little* nutmeg

Beat the butter and sugar well together till quite light and white, add the wine and nutmeg by degrees, and beat till thoroughly mixed.

Mrs. SANDBACH.

ROKEBY SAUCE (for Fish).

A gill of cream
1 oz. of butter
½ teaspoonful of soy sauce

½ teaspoonful of essence of anchovy
A few drops of Chilli vinegar

A few grains of cayenne pepper

Mix well together, and heat to boiling heat—but don't quite let it boil.

Miss CAMPBELL of Jura.

RUM BUTTER.

1 lb. of brown sugar
6 oz. of butter melted

1 small grated nutmeg
1 wine glassful of rum

Castor sugar to taste

Mix the sugar and nutmeg together, add the melted butter,
then the rum, and beat all well. Next pour the mixture
on to a dish and let it get cold, then sieve over it some
castor sugar, and serve with oatmeal biscuits.

Miss Hughes.

SALAD DRESSING FOR FOUR.

1 egg	½ teaspoonful sugar
2 saltspoonfuls salt	1 teaspoonful Tarragon vinegar
Cayenne pepper	1 teaspoonful salad vinegar
Tablespoonful best salad oil	2 tablespoonfuls cream

Whip all together, and pour over salad *just* before serving.
The vinegar and oil must be added very gradually in
drops. Mr. Gunn.

SALAD DRESSING.

Raw yolk of egg	1 teaspoonful of Tarragon vinegar
1 teaspoonful powdered sugar	1 pinch of salt

When well mixed add ½ teacupful cream.

Broadmeadows.

SHARP SAUCE (for Baked Fish).

Yolk of 1 egg	3 tablespoonfuls cream
1 tablespoonful vinegar	½ oz. butter
1 teaspoonful anchovy	Salt

Melt the butter, as soon as it boils add cream, yolk,
vinegar, anchovy, and salt. Do not let it boil again,
only warm up by the fire.

Mrs. Campbell of Inverneill.

SAUCE FOR COLD MEAT.

1 small pot red currant jelly	1 tablespoonful of mustard
Add a little water	The juice of a lemon

The peel of one orange cut fine

Mix well together.

Mrs. W. E. Crum.

TO PICKLE WALNUTS.

First blanch the walnuts, then put them in salt and water
for 2 days. Afterwards boil enough vinegar to cover
them, and put with the vinegar a few cloves and some
peppercorns. Put the walnuts in when boiling. Boil
them 4 times, at intervals of 10 days, then put them in a
jar. It improves them to prick them with a fork.

Mrs. Sandbach.

SAUCE FOR LIGHT PUDDING.

1 gill sherry		½ oz. castor sugar
½ gill water		1 tablespoonful apricot jam
	1 teaspoonful lemon juice	

Put all into a stewpan and let simmer 10 minutes, then strain and serve.

Miss A. PENNIFOLD,

32 Old Queen Street, Westminster.

SAUCE FOR WILD DUCK.

A little copper saucepan on a spirit lamp, for choice on the dinner table, with some good gravy in it.

Squeeze ½ or all the juice of a lemon according to quantity required, add ½ or all a wineglassful of port, and some cayenne pepper, very hot. Wild duck should be lightly roasted.

Colonel SANDBACH, Hafodunos.

ADDITIONAL RECIPES.

ADDITIONAL RECIPES.

Folklore and Mythology Archive

JAMS,
SWEETMEATS, Etc.

ALMOND ICING.

Put 2 lbs. loaf sugar and $\frac{1}{2}$ pint of water in stewpan, boil
(feather degree), add a few spots of yellow colouring, add
the $\frac{1}{4}$ lb. ground almonds.

Mr. Thomas Hill.

APPLE CHEESE (very good).

To every pound of apples (reduced to a pulp) allow 1 lb. powdered sugar	The grated rind and juice of 4 small lemons
	4 well-beaten eggs

1 oz. butter

Mix well all but the butter. Melt the latter in a stewpan,
add the other ingredients and stir over a moderate fire
till all the butter is thoroughly absorbed, then pour into
pots or moulds.

Mrs. W. E. Crum.

APPLE GINGER PASTE.

6 lb. baking apples	2 oz. whole ginger (steeped for 24 hours in whisky or ginger wine)
5 lb. cane sugar	
Rind and juice of 5 lemons	

Peel and core the apples, cover with cold water in a pan
and boil till soft, put the pulp through a sieve and add
the sugar and lemon rind and juice, and ginger. Boil all

together about an hour. Wet the moulds carefully and
fill up. Cover with paper and then it will keep quite
well. This quantity would make 4 shapes of medium
size.

Mrs. GEDDES,
St. John's Manse, Largs.

TO PRESERVE APRICOTS & GREENGAGES.

Equal weights of fruit and sugar. Choose the largest,
when they begin to soften, not too ripe. Split them
without paring (apricots must be pared). Strew part of
the sugar over them. Blanch the kernels with a small
sharp knife. Next day pour the syrup from the fruit and
boil it, with the other sugar, 6 or 8 minutes very gently.
Skim and add the plums and kernels. Then simmer till
clear, taking off any scum that rises; put the fruit singly
into small pots, and pour the syrup and kernels to it.

Mrs. W. E. CRUM.

CRYSTALLISED CURRANTS.

(These are very pretty for dessert.)

Take a nice spray of red currants, drag it through white
of egg (previously broken on to a plate and mixed well
but *not* beaten), then through *warmed* white sugar; dry in
the screen on a sieve.

Miss S. PILKINGTON,
Sandside, Caithness.

FRUIT JUICE.

Put 6 lbs. of fruit in a large flat dish. Sprinkle over it a
little powdered sugar, and 1 oz. of tartaric acid. Let it
stand 12 or more hours, then strain it into a large bowl.
To every pint (2 tumblers) put 1 lb. of sugar. Let it
stand till it is quite clear (it ferments) stirring every day.
Put into bottles and seal.

To MAKE INTO JELLY.—Melt ¾ oz. gelatine in a bowl and pour 1 pint of juice over it, stir well, and put into mould.

Mrs. W. E. CRUM.

TO BOTTLE GOOSEBERRIES.

Wash the gooseberries and fill the bottle with them. Fill up the bottles with cold water and a piece of alum the size of a pea. Fill a pan with water and put in the bottles. Let them steam till the gooseberries rise up a little from the bottom of the bottle. Then take them out and let them stand three days. Fill up the bottles with cold water that has been *boiled*, and seal with *oil* on the top of the water.

BROADMEADOWS, Selkirk.

MARMALADE. 1.

12 Seville oranges		Juice of 2 large lemons
4 sweet oranges		6 quarts water
	12 lbs. white sugar	

Cut the oranges in thin slices and put them to soak in the water for 24 hours. Then boil in the same water for 2 hours; boil the pips in a muslin bag with the rest, but take out before adding the sugar. Add sugar and boil another hour. Add the lemon juice, and boil now not more than another ½ hour. Will fill about 8 quart pots.

Mrs. BERTHON.

MARMALADE. 2.

An easy way.

| 7 bitter oranges | | 7 lbs. sugar |
| | 8 pints of water | |

Wash the oranges in warm water and scrape off black specks, if any. Then with a very sharp knife cut the oranges across in thin slices right through skin and pulp, the pips will fall out and they should be placed in a basin. Then recut the slices so that the pieces of peel are not too long; these should then be placed in a basin and add the 8 pints of cold water; place the pips in a muslin bag and let them soak in the water with the peel for 24 hours. Then place all together in a preserving pan and boil for 1½ hours without the sugar (when it has boiled for about 1 hour take out the bag of pips). Now add the sugar and boil for another ½ hour, fill up the pots and cover when cold.

Messrs. M. Campbell & Son,
Preserve Makers,
15 Hartington Place, Edinburgh.

MARRON BALLS (for 7 people).

| About ¾ lb. chestnuts | | Whipped cream |
| Castor sugar | | Angelica |

Mix the chestnuts to a pulp in the mortar, add sugar till you get the right consistency, make into balls, glacé with sugar* " to the crack," serve with cream, and stalks made of angelica in each ball.

* 1 lb. lump sugar, let it boil, try it in cold water; when it breaks crisply (" cracks ") it is ready.

Miss S. Pilkington, Sandside.

MARROW JAM.

A marrow		Lemons
Sugar		Bruised ginger
	Chillies	

Peel the marrow, removing all soft parts and seeds. Cut into squares of about an inch. To 1 lb. of marrow add an equal weight of sugar, and to every 4 lbs. of marrow add the juice and thin rind of 2 lemons. Mix these all together, and let all stand for 24 hours. Then add 1 oz. of bruised ginger and 9 or 10 chillies (in a muslin bag). Boil for 1½ hours, stirring and skimming continually.

Mrs. James Tinne,
Bashley Lodge, New Forest.

ORANGE BISCUITS.

Boil whole Seville oranges in two or three waters till most of the bitterness is gone ; cut them and take out the pulp and juice; then beat the outside very fine in a mortar, and put to it an equal weight of fine sifted sugar. When extremely well mixed to a paste, spread it thin on china dishes and set them in the sun or before the fire ; when half dry, cut up in cakes and turn other side up to dry.

BEECHWOOD.

ORANGES ICED.

(A pretty Christmas dish.)

Take some nice oranges, carefully peel them and remove the white skin without breaking the skin of the orange ; then put a knitting needle through the centre of the orange and dip it (the orange) in a basin of icing flavoured with orange flavouring, and hold it before the fire to set, when it should look pearly or like ice ; place on dish with imitation holly leaves ; it makes a very nice table ornament.

ICING FOR ORANGES.—2 whites of eggs, $\frac{1}{2}$ lb. icing sugar, beaten to a froth.

Mr. THOMAS HILL.

PEPPERMINT CREAMS.

| 1 lb. icing sugar | 1 teaspoonful of water |
| White of 1 egg | 15 drops of oil of peppermint |

Knead the sugar well with the white of egg, which you have beaten a little, and into which you have dropped the peppermint oil ; add the teaspoonful of water by degrees, roll out evenly and cut with small cutter ; lay out in a tray for 24 hours to dry a little and keep in tin box.   Do not roll too thin, but rather thicker than a penny piece.   No cooking is necessary.

Mrs. GEORGE BROWN,
Châlet Fairlie, Pau.

PINEAPPLE DROPS.

Bruise the pulp of a very ripe pineapple in a mortar, and pass through a coarse hair sieve. Add sufficient cane sugar to make into a stiff paste. Boil this in a sugar boiler, and then let it fall in drops on to an oiled baking sheet. When cold place in a sieve in a hot screen till dry.

Coypright, by kind permission of the WEST INDIAN PRODUCE ASSOCIATION, Ltd., 4 Fenchurch Buildings, London, E.C.

UNCOOKED RASPBERRY JAM.

Mash down the fresh raspberries with a silver fork, and allow one pound and a quarter of castor sugar for each pound of fruit. Heat the fruit as hot as possible before the fire, and have the sugar red hot (but not browned) in the oven in flat dishes ; mix all well together and have the pots red hot. Tie down *at once* with butter papers and fine string.

It takes three people to make this jam, and everything must be ready before beginning to mix.

ROBERT CUNNINGHAM, Esq.
Eddesbury, West Derby.

RASPBERRY JAM (without boiling).

1 lb. granulated sugar to each pound of raspberries. Put the sugar into the oven to heat through thoroughly, look at it from time to time to keep it from caking or browning. Put the fruit into an earthenware jar over the fire to warm thoroughly; when heated, remove from the fire and mash the fruit into a pulp, then add the hot sugar and stir or beat briskly for 5 minutes. Cover and let it stand for half an hour, heat again, and stir or beat for 5 minutes, stand half an hour, once again beat for 5 minutes, put into pots and cover. In all beaten 15 minutes.

Mrs. W. CALDERWOOD, 7 East Castle Road, Edinburgh.

ROWAN JELLY.

| Rowan berries | | Loaf sugar |

Gather the berries just as they are on the point of being ripe, rinse them in water, and put them in a jelly pan with enough water to cover them. Boil till the berries are soft, then strain the liquor through a bag and return it to the fire. Add a pound of loaf sugar to every pint of juice, and boil rapidly for half-an-hour, simmering carefully.

Miss L. M'INROY of Lude.

RUSSIAN TOFFEE. 1.

6d. worth cream		¼ teacupful treacle
Whites 2 eggs		Small piece of butter
2 lbs. brown sugar		1 teaspoonful vanilla

Beat the white of eggs separately, add all other ingredients except the vanilla, which should be added just before pouring into the tins.

Mrs. W. E. CRUM.

RUSSIAN TOFFEE. 2.

1 lb. moist brown sugar		A cupful golden syrup (treacle
½ (or ¼ lb.) butter		is better, or both mixed)
4 oz. grated chocolate		A cupful of cream (or partly
2 oz. blanched almonds		milk)

First grate the chocolate and blanch the almonds. Put the butter in a saucepan to melt. Then add the other ingredients—omitting the almonds—boil for 20 minutes, stirring all the time; then put half the almonds in, and boil for 10 minutes longer. Try on a plate, and if found not firm boil a little longer. Put on a buttered plate, and arrange the remainder of the almonds in patterns while the toffee is hot.

The chocolate can be broken into small pieces instead of grating.

Or you may use ½ lb. white sifted sugar and ½ lb. brown.

BEECHWOOD.

WHOLE STRAWBERRY JAM.

7 lbs. fruit | 7 lbs. loaf sugar
1 teacupful water

Put a teacupful of water into the jelly pan, and dissolve in this some sugar first. Then put in *small quantities* of sugar and fruit time about; this gradually dissolves the sugar and helps to keep the fruit whole; bring to the boil, and keep boiling moderately for ¾-of-an-hour. The fruit should be gathered when dry, and be perfectly fresh. The longer it is boiled the thicker it gets, but this takes from the flavour of the jam.

Use gummed and wax tissues combined to cover, and keep in a dry place.

Miss JANET FIFE, Fairlie.

TO CLARIFY SUGAR.

1 lb. best lump sugar | 1 pint water

Place on a slow fire till it comes to the boil, clear off the scum, but don't stir it up except once or so to mix it, and allow to stand till cold before pouring over the fruit.

Mrs. CAMPBELL of Inverneill.

TOFFEE.

1 lb. sugar (moist) | A few drops of vanilla,
½ lb. butter | or better, a table-
1 lb. golden syrup | spoonful of vinegar.

Melt the butter in a large pan, add the sugar, and stir over the fire till melted; then add the golden syrup, stirring all the time, and let it boil, never stopping stirring. To tell when finished drop a little in a cup of water, when cool it should be perfectly crisp when bitten. Just before the toffee is done throw in the vinegar and stir briskly.

Pour on to dishes greased with a little butter, and break up when cold.

Mrs. F. BATESON, Bell Farm,
Clewer, Windsor.

WATER ICING.

| 2 lbs. icing sugar | | ¼ oz. tartaric acid |

Add boiling water to make into a soft paste, then give it a good beating up with a wooden spatula. The more you beat it the better it will look and set.

Mr. THOMAS HILL.

ADDITIONAL RECIPES.

ADDITIONAL RECIPES.

T. & R. ANNAN & SONS.

GENERAL PHOTOGRAPHERS.
FINE ART PUBLISHERS.
BOOK ILLUSTRATORS.

At Messrs. ANNAN'S new establishment a very fine Portrait Studio has been erected on the top of the building, with a commodious hydraulic lift from the ground floor.

A complete set of the firm's publications in Autotype, of reproductions from Important Pictures, may be seen in the Gallery.

518 SAUCHIEHALL STREET,
CHARING CROSS,
GLASGOW.

INVALID COOKERY.

ARROWROOT GRUEL.

Arrowroot		Water
Brandy		Sugar to taste
	½ or ¼ pint of cream	

Put the usual quantity of arrowroot into a cup, mix it with water enough to make it smooth (and the usual quantity of brandy if allowed). Then pour in boiling water and add sugar. Last of all, just before eating, pour in and mix ½ or ¼ of a pint of cream. The arrowroot is better for being boiled up before adding the cream.

A Doctor's Recipe.

ARROWROOT PUDDING.

½ pint of milk		1 dessertspoonful arrowroot mixed
1 egg		with milk
	1 oz. of castor sugar	

Boil the milk and pour it on to the arrowroot and put back into the saucepan and boil a few minutes, stir in the sugar, add the yolk of egg, whip white to a stiff froth and stir in, butter a pie dish, pour the mixture in and bake 10 minutes.

Miss Reed.

BARLEY WATER.

1 tablespoonful pearl barley		Rind of 1 lemon
1 or 2 lumps of sugar		Juice of ½ a lemon
	1 quart boiling water	

Wash the barley in cold water, add the sugar, lemon rind, and juice, pour on the boiling water, let it stand in a cool place for 3 or 4 hours, then strain for use through a fine hair sieve.

Mrs. W. E. Crum.

EGG JELLY.

½ oz. gelatine	1 egg
2 oz. sugar	Water
1 lemon	1 lump of sugar

Rub the lump of sugar on the lemon rind, then put it with the gelatine, sugar, and ¼ pint water into a saucepan, and stir over the fire till dissolved. Squeeze the juice from the lemon, and add sufficient water to make up a quarter of a pint, add this and the beaten yolk of egg to the ingredients in saucepan, bring to the boil, remove from the fire, add the stiffly beaten whites and pour into moulds.

Miss REED, Horsham.

QUICKLY-MADE BEEF TEA.

Beef chopped as finely as possible, and quite freed from fat, and soaked in its own weight of water for 10 minutes or so. Then heat to boiling point, let it boil for 2 or 3 minutes and you will have a strong delicious beef tea, better than can be made by boiling in the ordinary way many hours.

Mrs. SANDBACH.

BEEF TEA.

1 lb. beef	1 to 1½ pints water

Shred the beef, add half pint cold water, put in a jar and stand in a saucepan of cold water. Bring the water to a quick boil and then simmer for 3 or 4 hours, then strain off the beef tea and add 1 or ½ a pint boiling water to the beef again, and stand it in boiling water to simmer for 2 or 3 hours. Then add it to first strainings and let it stand; skim before using.

Mrs. W. E. CRUM.

THREE MEAT TEA.

2 lb. of gravy beef from the leg	An old hen, cut up very small
2 lb. of gravy veal	bones and all
2 quarts (or 3 pints) of cold water	A little salt

Simmer very slowly for 8 hours, strain through a cloth and skim off any scum there may be.

Miss GRAHAM, Sen.,
20 Allan Park, Stirling.

BULLOCK'S HEEL AND MILK.

Get a bullock's heel, have it well scraped and cleaned, put into a quart of milk and let it simmer till it is a pint. One bullock's heel will do twice. This is very nice warm to drink, or cold as a jelly.

Miss GRAHAM, Sen.

VERY STRONG CHICKEN JELLY.

Skin a chicken, cut up and place in a basin of water (only for a minute or so). Lift each piece out with whatever water clings to it, place in a double saucepan, and cook for $3\frac{1}{2}$ to 4 hours (till the flesh crumbles off the bones). Then take out the bits of chicken and strain the liquid through muslin, or a hair sieve, season (if allowed) with pepper and salt, and remove fat while hot with tissue paper. A jar placed in a saucepan of water does quite as well as a double saucepan.

Miss JONES,
1 Hoscote Park, West Kirby.

FOR A COUGH.

Roast a lemon very carefully, without burning it ; when it is thoroughly hot, cut and squeeze it into a cup, upon 3 oz. pounded sugar. Take a tablespoonful when the cough is troublesome, or add boiling water and take it hot.

Miss GRAHAM, Sen.

LEMON WHEY.

½ pint milk | Juice of ½ lemon
A little sifted sugar

Roll the lemon to make it juicy, then cut in half and squeeze into the boiling milk which had been put on the fire in a small saucepan. Don't use a lemon squeezer. Be careful not to let the pips fall into the milk, as it spoils the flavour. Boil the milk and lemon for about one minute, when it will curdle. Then strain into a basin. Add the sugar. Take cold or hot.

Mrs. W. E. CRUM.

MEAT JELLY.

1 lb. of veal, 1 lb. of beef without any | 2 wineglassfuls of good
fat, cut up in small pieces | brandy

Put the meat and brandy in a jar with a cover, and stand it in a pan of boiling water, and let it boil for 4 hours. Then strain through muslin.

Mrs. W. E. CRUM.

MILK GRUEL.

Oatmeal | Sugar to taste
Boiling milk | 2 tablespoonfuls of cream
2 tablespoonfuls of brandy

Strain a sufficient quantity of oatmeal with hot milk. Squeeze it to get all the good out of the oatmeal. Have ready a cup of boiling milk, when it is quite boiling pour what you have strained from the oatmeal into it and boil again till there is no raw taste in it. Stir it well while boiling. Add sugar, and mix in 2 tablespoonfuls of cream. If allowed add two tablespoonfuls brandy. It should be almost thin enough to drink.

Mrs. W. E. CRUM.

RESTORATIVE JELLY, 1.

3 oz. isinglass | 3 oz. white sugar candy
1 oz. gum arabic | 1 pint port wine
1 nutmeg grated fine.

Put all in a jar tied up close, and simmer 12 hours in a pan of water. Then strain through a piece of muslin.

Mrs. W. E. CRUM.

RESTORATIVE JELLY. 2.

| 2 lbs. lean veal | | 2 turnips sliced |

Put alternative layers of veal and turnip into a mug. Tie it up close, set in a pan of water over a slow fire, let it stew about 2 hours, then strain it. It will go into a jelly when cold, and can be eaten thus, or two tablespoonfuls in a small tea-cup of hot water.

Mrs. SANDBACH.

DR. CHAPNELL'S SOUP FOR INVALIDS.

I lb. beef		1 lb. neck of mutton
1 lb. veal		1 calf's foot
	1 pint of water	

Simmer for 6 hours, skim carefully and season.

DR. WILLIAMS' INVALID SOUP.

Shin of beef, 4 or 5 lbs.		2 quarts water
Knuckle of veal, 4 or 5 lbs. (or		A few carrots and onions
if not possible to get veal		A little arrowroot
replace with mutton)		If liked a little wine

Put the meat in a digester with 2 quarts of water. Boil 4 hours, add the vegetables, boil another hour, strain off. Next day remove the fat and thicken with arrowroot, add a little wine if liked. It may be taken cold as a jelly or warm as a soup.

STEAMED INVALID'S PUDDING.

| ½ pint of milk | | A slice of stale bread |
| 1 egg | | sugar and flavouring to taste. |

Break the bread in a basin, pour over it boiling milk; cover it and let it stand a little; beat it with a fork and add the beaten egg and sugar. Steam 20 minutes in a buttered basin or bake. Lemon peel or peach leaves, boiled in the milk, make a nice flavouring.

Miss REED.

STRENGTHENING MIXTURE
FOR WEAK CHEST.

4 unbroken eggs laid in a basin, with juice of 4 lemons squeezed over, and quite covered with a plate. In 24 hours a good deal of lime from the shells will be dissolved. Then take out the eggs, beat them thoroughly and add very gradually, beating all the time, $\frac{1}{2}$ pint new milk (previously boiled and allowed to get cold), $\frac{1}{2}$ pound or less of powdered loaf sugar, and $\frac{1}{2}$ pint of old rum. Last of all strain the lime and lemon juice through a strainer. Add *very slowly* the ingredients that have been beaten together; it will be about the consistency of a custard. Bottle and cork tightly.

DOSE.—1 Tablespoonful taken early in the morning, with a little hot water if preferred.

It is also a good tonic.

Miss BURT,
6 Downshire Hill, Hampstead, N.W.

ADDITIONAL RECIPES.

David Nutt,

57-59 LONG ACRE, LONDON.

M R. NUTT begs to call attention to the facilities which he can offer for the supply of all foreign works (French, German, Italian, Spanish, etc., etc.), in all departments of LITERATURE, ART, HISTORY and NATURAL SCIENCE. His Stock, which is the largest in the Kingdom, is continually being replenished.

**LISTS AND CATALOGUES ARE SENT ON APPLICATION.
SUBSCRIPTIONS ARE TAKEN TO ALL FOREIGN PERIODICALS.**

Mr. Nutt begs to call special attention to his Library of French Writers, in which the best standard works of classical and modern French Literature are to be had **in an attractive and durable binding**, at a price little superior to that of the unbound volumes. A List will be sent to you on application.

Mr. Nutt has published a large number of works for the study of the Language, Literature, and History of the Celtic Peoples, especially the Gaels of Ireland and Scotland. A full List of his Celtic Publications will be sent on application. In particular, Mr. Nutt issues the publications of the *Irish Texts Society* and of the *Folk Lore Society,* so many of which are concerned with Celtic matters. Prospectuses of both Societies, with full Lists of their Publications, sent on application.

To Students of early Irish History and Literature Mr. Nutt can strongly recommend the works of Miss ELEANOR HULL: Early Pagan Ireland, 2/6; Early Christian Ireland, 2/6; Early Irish Literature, 3/6.

GAELIC RECIPES.

BREACAGAN BLASDA.

| 1 phunnd de Mhìn-mhìn Ullaichte | 2 ùnnsa Siùcair |
| 2 ùnnsa Ime | 1 Ugh. |

Cuir an t-iomlan ann an soitheach agus sloistir le
blàthaich gus am bi agad taois thana a ruitheas á spain
air a'ghreideal. Ma chi thu 'nuair tha na bonnaichean
deas, gu bheil iad tuille's tiugh, dean an taois na's buige.

Le ugh eile, agus uachdar, no bainne blàth math a
chur an aite blàthaich, bithidh na bonnaichean fior
bhlasda, ged a bhitheas iad car cosdail.

(*Translation.*)
BANNOCK SCONES.

| 1 lb. prepared (or patent) flour | 2 oz. sugar |
| 2 oz. butter | 1 egg |

Put all into a basin and work up with buttermilk into a
stiff batter which can be dropped on a girdle with a
spoon. If, when fired, they are too thick, this can be
remedied by making the batter softer.

By the addition of one egg extra, and worked up with
thick cream, or even pure warm milk, instead of buttermilk, it makes a most delicious, though somewhat
expensive, scone.

CARAICEAGAN.

| ½ phunnd de Mhìn-mhìn Ullaichte | 1 ùnnsa Ime (air a leaghadh). |
| 3 ùnnsachan Siùcair | 2 Ugh |

Sloistir an t-iomlan le blàthaich agus oibrich e gus am
bi agad taois ro thana. Leig leis an taois ruith ás an
spàin air a' ghreideal. 'Nuair a tha an taobh tha fodha
donn tionndaidh an taobh eile fodha le sgèin. 'Nuair tha
iad deas cha bu chòir dhaibh a bhi thar ceathramh an
òirlich air tiughad, agus bu chòir an taois a bhi air a
riaghailteachadh do reir so.

(Translation).

PANCAKES.

½ lb. prepared flour | 1 oz. butter (previously melted).
3 oz. sugar | 2 eggs

Mix these with buttermilk and work up into a smooth, soft batter. Drop the batter on the girdle with a spoon. When nicely browned, turn the cakes with a knife. When finished they should not be over a quarter of an inch in thickness, and the softness of the batter should be regulated accordingly.

CARAICEAGAN-TANA.

9 ùnnsachan Min-mhin Ullaichte | 1 ùnnsa Ime
3 Uighean | 4 ùnnsachan Siùcair

Cuir so uile ann an soitheach agus measgaich gu h-iomlan le bláthaich, no cè (uachdar) tiugh, gus am bi agad taois ro thana, teann air cho tana ri easach. Leig leis an taois ruith á spàin air a' ghreideal uiread 's a tha feumail ; sgaoilidh e glé thana. 'Nuair a tha an darna taobh donn tionndaidh e le sgèin, agus donn an taobh eile. 'Nuair a tha iad deas cha bu chòir dhaibh a bhi thar an cóigeamh cuid de dh' òirleach air tiughad. Ma ghabhas tu na caraiceagan 'nuair tha iad deas, agus an sgaoileadh thairis le slamban mheasan no siùcar, agus an deanamh 'nan rolag, bithidh iad eireachdail mar dheireannan.

Air neo, gabh poiteag-charaiceag agus cuir innte leth-spain-tea de dh' im, cuir air an teine i gus am bi i *fuathasach teth*, agus dòirt innte cuid de 'n taois, crath a' phoiteag thar an teine, a chumail a suas an teas ; 'nuair a tha an darna taobh deas, tionndaidh an taobh eile fodha. 'Nuair a tha e bruich bithidh an t-im uile sùighte ; cuir a nis air trinnsear e, crath deannag shiùcair air agus crathadh beag de dhinnsear agus riaraich 'nuair tha e teth.

(Translation.)

CRUMPETS.

9 oz. prepared flour | 1 oz. butter
3 eggs | 4 oz. sugar

Put all the above into a basin and mix thoroughly with buttermilk or thick cream, and reduce it to a soft batter something like gruel.   Pour on the girdle with a ladle the quantity you require; it will spread out very thin. When sufficiently fired on one side turn it over with a knife and brown the other side.   When finished, these should not be above one fifth of an inch in thickness.   If you take the above when fired and spread over with jelly or sugar and roll them up tightly in paper till they set, they will make an excellent dessert.

Or again, take an omelet pan, and put into it half a teaspoonful of butter, heat it on the fire till *very hot*, and pour some of the above batter into it.   Shake the pan over the fire to keep up the heat; when fired on one side, turn over.   When cooked it will have absorbed all the butter; throw it on to a plate, dust it with sugar, sprinkle a little ground ginger over it, and serve it hot.

SGRATH-BREATHACH AOTROM.

1 phunnd Min-mhìn Chaoin		1 phunnd Ime
	Uisge	

Dinn an t-im am measg na min-mhìn agus geàrr na th' ann 'na mhìrean beaga cruinne, mu mheudachd ceann na h-òrdaige : dean toll beag na mheadhon agus cuir uisge ann.   Dean taois de 'n mhin-mhìn 's de 'n t-im, gun an t-im a bhruthadh.   Crath min-mhìn orra agus sgaoil a mach iad leis a' chrann-arain, cuir.crathadh eile orra ; fill thairis iad agus sgaoil a mach iad a dhà no tri uairean. Tuigidh tu ann an ùine ghoirid cia meud uair a dh' fheumar an sgaoileadh a mach.

(*Translation.*)
LIGHT PUFF PASTE.

1 lb. soft flour		1 lb. butter
	Water	

Press the butter flat amongst the flour, and cut it into small pieces the size of a marble ; form a small hole in the centre and add water.   Dough up the flour and butter with the hand without bruising the butter.   Dust over and press out with rolling pin.   Dust again ; fold over and press out two or three times.   Experience will determine the number of times to be given.

CLAR SIÙCAIR.

2 phunnd Siùcair | ¼ lb. Ime
3 cupain Uisge

Leagh an siucar anns an uisge ; cha dean gràinne no dhà de shiùcar gun leaghadh coire dha. Cuir an t-im anns a' phoit, ach na goil e cho bras 's a ni thu 'nuair is e siùcaran righinn a th' air t' aire. Feuch am bheil e ullamh mar a ni thu le siùcaran righinn, agus 'nuair a dh' fhàsas e cho tiugh ri taois, tog bhàrr an teine e. Fàg blasda e le brìghean milis. Ma' s e dinnsear pronn a tha thu cur ann fóghnaidh fior bheagan, agus bu chòir a leaghadh ann an uisge an toiseach. Bu chòir do'n iomlan a bhi nis air a ghrad chur mu'n cuairt le spàin. Toisichidh e ri fàs cruaidh mu na h-oirean ; ach sgrìob so dheth uair is uair, agus cum mu 'n cuairt e gus am bi e garbh gu leòir. An sin taom e air lic a chaidh a shuathadh le im. Ma tha e tuille 's garbh cha dòirt e mach réidh ; air an laimh eile ma tha e tuille's bog bithidh e leanailteach. Thig teòmachd le cleachdadh.

(*Translation.*)

SUGAR TABLET.

2 lb. sugar | ¼ lb. butter
3 cups water

Dissolve the sugar in the water ; a few grains of unmelted sugar will not spoil this tablet. Add the butter, but do not boil so high as when making toffy. Test as when making toffy, and when it has assumed the consistency of soft putty take it off the fire. Add flavouring or essence according to taste. If ground ginger be used a small quantity will suffice ; it should be dissolved in a little water before being used. The mass should now be stirred quickly with a spoon. It will begin to solidify round the edge, scrape this off repeatedly and keep stirring till the mass is sufficiently grained, Then pour on to a buttered slab. If too high grained it will not pour out flat ; on the other hand, if too thin it will be sticky. Practice will overcome any difficulty in this respect.

Messrs. Lafayette, Ltd., have been appointed Official Photographers to the Bazaar.

ADDITIONAL RECIPES.

Folklore and Mythology Archive

MISCELLANEOUS.

ASPIC JELLY.

2 oz. Marshall's gelatine	2 whites and shells of eggs
1 quart hot water	Small teacup white tarragon vinegar
1 dessertspoonful salt	One onion sliced
One or two bay leaves	20 peppercorns and allspice mixed

Put all the ingredients into a stewpan and place on the
stove, and when it comes to the boil, pass it through a
hot wet jelly bag or cloth.

Mrs. JAMES TINNE,
Bashley Lodge, New Forest.

CREAM CHEESE.

1 pint cream, just made warm, a small piece of rennet to
turn it, to be hung up in muslin for about 2 days, and
pressed for one day.

Miss S. SANDBACH,
Cherry Hill, Malpas, Cheshire.

CROWDIE.

To one quart of milk one dessertspoonful rennet. Milk
must be lukewarm. Set for 20 minutes, then stir.
Crowdie will fall to the bottom. Put in to a colander and
strain for 2 hours until quite dry. Then mix with cream
and salt to taste.

Mrs. DARROCH of Torridon.

DELICIOUS SANDWICH-FILLINGS.

Celery put through the mincing machine and mixed with a little mayonnaise.

Celery and mayonnaise, with a little finely chopped chicken or veal added.

Cold boiled green peas, mashed and mixed with a little salad dressing.

Thinly sliced cucumber, and beef, and a suspicion of mayonnaise.

Miss STIRLING,
Gargunnock, Stirling.

Brown bread with whipped cream and chopped celery.

ICES.

1 pint milk	Sugar to taste
Yolks of 2 and white of 1 egg	Jam
1 pint cream	

Make a custard of the eggs, sugar, and milk, mix the jam with it *in the freezer*, as they will curdle if allowed to stand before freezing. Freeze a few minutes, then add the whipped cream, and freeze (about 20 minutes is usually enough).

With fresh fruit use only cream and sugar, no custard.

For water ices use about 1 gill syrup or fruit purée to 1 pint water; tkey take less time than cream ices to freeze.

ITALIAN CHEESE.

| 2 gills of sour cream | The juice of 1 lemon |
| 2 oz. pounded sugar | 1 white of egg |

Beat all together for ten minutes, then pour in muslin in a thick strainer, so that the juice may run out of it, but not the cream; the next day turn it out and serve without sauce.

Mrs. W. E. CRUM.

"PATENT FLOUR."

To avoid trouble and waste of time in weighing small quantities of carbonate of soda and cream of tartar for ærating cakes, &c., this "Patent" flour will be found useful.

14 lb. best flour		6 oz. cream of tartar
	3 oz. carbonate of soda	

Mix all together and put through a fine sieve, twice or three times to well mix ; keep in a dry place for use.

Mr. Thomas Hill,
12 Gladstone Road, Seacombe.

PUTTENHAM CHEESE.

1 egg		3 oz. cheese

Beat all up together and bake 10 minutes.

Mrs. Sandbach.

RECIPE FOR SEASONING.

½ lb white pepper		½ oz. mace
½ oz. nutmegs		½ oz. cayenne

Pound all well together and put into a bottle for use.

Mrs. Campbell of Inverneill.

RECIPE FOR PREVENTING MILK TASTING OF TURNIPS.

As soon as the milk is brought into the dairy pour into it boiling water, in the proportion of ½ a pint to a gallon of milk, cover it over with a cloth 4 times doubled, for ½ an hour, then strain and pour into milk dishes.

N.B.—Never put a wooden cover instead of a cloth over the milk pail.

Mrs. Sandbach.

SOWENS. Lagan or Cabhruich.)

A peck of good pronn, and pour tepid water over it, and let it lie for two or three days, and strain as you use it. Boil till it is as thick as porridge, stirring all the time.

Mrs. BEATON, Essich.

TO CLEAN INDIAN BRASS TRAYS.

Wood ashes and lemon juice and then held under a tap of water and well rubbed.

Mrs. CAMPBELL of Inverneill.

CURE FOR CHILBLAINS.

(This causes instant relief, but must not be used for *broken* chilblains.)

Plunge the affected parts in water *as hot as you can possibly bear it*, for 3 minutes (adding hotter water as the other cools), then plunge them into stone-cold water for 3 minutes, repeat, and you will find all irritation has gone.

It is as well to time oneself by a watch, as it is important to count the full 3 minutes.

ANCIENT COOKERY.

The following recipes are at least 500 years old, and probably much older.

RAFFYOLIS.

Take swynes lire, and sethe hit, and hewe hit smalle, and do therto zolkes of egges, and medel hit wel togedur, ande make hit right souple, ande do therto a lytel larde mynced, and grated chese, and pouder of ginger, and of canelle ; then take and make balles therof as gret as an appull, and wynde hom in the calle of the swyne, every balle by hymself; then make a coffyn of paste schapet aftur hit, and lay hit therin, and bake hit; and when thai byn baken, take zolkes of egges, and bete hom welle in a vessel, and do therto sugur, ande gode pouder, and colour hit with saffron, and pour above, and serve hit forthe.

CREM BOYLED.

Take crem of cowe mylke, and zolkes of egges, and bete hom wel togedur, and do hit in a pot, and let hit boyle tyl hit be stondynge, and do therto sugur, and colour hit with saffron, and dresse hit forthe in leches, and plante therin floures of borage, or of vyolet.

PAYN RAGUN.

Take clarified honey, and sugur cypre, and boyle hom togedur with esy fire, that hit brenne not, and when hit hase boylet awhile take up a drope, and do hit in a lytel watur, and loke if it honge togedur; then take hit from the fyre, and do therto a gret quantitie of pynes, and pouder of ginger, and stere hit well togeder tyl hit begynne to thik; then take and cast hit on a wete table, and leche hit, and serve hit forthe with roste on flesh day, or fried mete on fish day.

VERT SAUSE.

Take parsel, and myntes, and peletur, and costmaryn, and sauge, and a lytel garlek and bredde, and grinde hit smal, and tempur hit up with vynegur, and do therto pouder of pepur, and of gynger, and of canel, and serve hit forthe.

GAUNSELL FOR GESE.

Take floure, and tempur hit with gode cowe mylke, and make hit thynne, and colour hit with saffron; and take garlek, and stamp hit, and do therto, and boyle hit, and serve hit forthe.

At a Feeste Roiall Pecokkes shall be dight on this manere.

Take and flee off the skynne with the fedurs tayle and the nekke, and the hed theron ; then take the skyn with all the fedurs, and lay hit on a table abrode ; and strawe theron grounden comyn ; then take the pecokke, and roste hym, and endore hym with rawe zolkes of egges ; and when he is rosted take hym of, and let hym coole awhile, and take and sowe hym in his skyn, and gilde his combe, and so serve hym forthe with the last cours.

Folklore and Mythology Archive

ADDITIONAL RECIPES.

ADDITIONAL RECIPES.

ADDITIONAL RECIPES.

Hints for Beginners.

Bicarbonate of soda turns cakes or puddings brown ; baking powder keeps them light in colour.

Never put macaroni into boiling water or it will go starchy ; put it in cold water and let it boil.

Salmon should always be put into boiling water as it keeps the colour better, but white fish should be put into cold water. Always put in salt *before* the fish, otherwise it breaks the skin.

Ices made with fresh fruit require less freezing than those made with jam ; the sweeter the ice the longer it takes to freeze.

The yolk of an egg will keep for a day or two, if not broken, and covered with water, or white of egg.

White of egg is best beaten in a clean brass pan, and standing in a draught. A pinch of salt sometimes helps.

In beating anything always accelerate the pace if you alter it, never retard.

Never use a knife or metal whisk with *heated* lemon ; it will not give it any taste if the lemon is *cold*.

Never let an iron whisk or spoon *stand* in coffee cream, or it will turn it black.

It is better not to use a tin mould for creams, as the soldering frequently discolours them.

Always make a hole in the paste of a meat pie before cooking, or you may very probably be poisoned.

In making soup only add the vegetables 2 hours before the soup has finished cooking.

When *isinglass* is given in recipes double the quantity of *gelatine* may be used instead.

Be careful not to bang the oven door in baking a cake or soufflé, as it will fall.

Breadsauce is improved by boiling the milk before putting in the crumbs.

A few sprigs of woodruff are a great improvement to claret or moselle cup.

Some cooks say the secret of making light soufflés is to put *no* flour in them.

In making coffee be sure to warm first the receptacle in which it is made, just as you would a teapot in making tea.

Many French cooks dip a (clean !) red-hot poker for one second into coffee just before serving, as this gives it the burnt flavour some people like.

Milk should actually be boiling when added to coffee.

To improve frozen game lay the birds in a bath of milk for 24 hours, changing the milk twice. Then roast in the ordinary way.

A separate pan should always be kept for boiling eggs and should be used for *nothing* else, or the results may be disastrous.

The way to boil all hard vegetables and dried fruit (if they have not been soaked the day before) is to add every now and then a tablespoonful of cold water.

"To cook *slowly* (except in a few exceptional cases) is the secret of all good cooking."

Hints on Jam Making.

The fruit should be freshly gathered on a *dry* day.

The preserving pan should be of brass, copper, or enamelled.

Be careful to clean the pans thoroughly before and after using, especially if made of brass or copper.

A silver or enamelled ladle should be used for filling the pots; if neither are at hand a breakfast cup will do.

In boiling both jams and jellies the spoon (wooden) should not be lifted off the bottom of the pan, otherwise the pan is liable to burn and the fruit to break up.

Jams should be boiled quickly over a strong fire and not allowed to simmer slowly, as it greatly depends on this whether the jams " set " or not.

When making jam never guess at quantities or weights, always follow out recipes to the letter.

M. CAMPBELL & SON,
Preserve Makers,
15 Hartington Place, Edinburgh.

"DIDO."

Folklore and Mythology Archive

INDEX.

Also Published by Kalevala Books

The Piper Came to Our Town:
Bagpipe Folklore, Legends, and Fairy Tales

Edited by Joanne Asala

The bagpipes have a long and noble history stretching back centuries. They have been played across Scotland, Ireland, Continental Europe, and the Middle East, and are found in such diverse places as India and the Americas. *The Piper Came to Our Town* is a collection of over seventy stories, tales, anecdotes, and legends of pipers, running the gamut from the ordinary to the supernatural. You will travel from the battlefields of Africa to faerie caves below the earth, and meet pipers urging troops to victory, fighting off man-eating cows, and even creating new worlds. *The Piper Came to Our Town* will delight fans of bagpipe music, lore, and tradition, as well as anyone who likes a good folk story.

ISBN-13: 978-1-880954-03-4

Historic Cookbooks of the World